SUSHI ᴧND TAPAS

Enjoy !

(p.53 essay)

FOREWORD BY HELEN CLARK

Sushi
and
Tapas

Bite-size personal stories
from women around the world

Edited by
PEPUKAYE BARDOUILLE and **NEO GIM HUAY**

EPIGRAM BOOKS / SINGAPORE

Published in Singapore by Epigram Books
www.epigrambooks.sg

Cover design by Stefany

National Library Board,
Singapore Cataloguing-in-Publication Data

Sushi and tapas : bite-size personal stories from women around
the world / edited by Pepukaye Bardouille and Neo Gim Huay;
foreword by Helen Clark. – Singapore : Epigram Books, 2012.

p. cm.
ISBN : 978-981-07-2818-2 (pbk.)

1. Women – Biography. I. Bardouille, Pepukaye.
II. Neo, Gim Huay.

HQ1155
920.72 -- dc23 OCN796975431

This is a re-publication of a work of the same title originally
self-published by Pepukaye Bardouille and Neo Gim Huay in 2011.

10 9 8 7 6 5 4 3 2 1

To Raj, my mother, teacher, agitator and empath
PB

To my nieces, Sze Min and Yi Teng,
our next generation
NGH

There is only one true form of wealth,
that of human contact.
– Antoine de Saint-Exupéry

CONTENTS

Foreword

It is a basic human right for women to enjoy full legal equality and equality of opportunity. Our societies are poorer if we fail to tap the full potential of half our populations. I advocate for the empowerment of women and the advancement of women in leadership around the world in my role as Administrator of the United Nations Development Programme. I bring to that advocacy my personal experience as Prime Minister of New Zealand for nine years, Leader of the Opposition for six years before that, Leader of the New Zealand Labour Party for fifteen years, and Member of Parliament in New Zealand for twenty-seven years. I am well-acquainted with the challenges women face when living and working in male-dominated arenas. What has kept me going is my determination to make a contribution to public life and to building more equal and just societies. I am fortunate indeed to have been able to pursue the career of my choice, and now to be able to work for better lives for women, men and children around the world. The twenty-five stories in this book draw from the experiences of women in many countries. They range from Sweden to South Africa, Japan to the United States, and Britain to China. Across diverse contexts, women are seen to share many experiences. In this way, this book builds bonds between us all. It is transformative in encouraging us to support the empowerment of women everywhere.

Helen Clark
Administrator, United Nations Development Programme,
Chair, United Nations Development Group and
former Prime Minister of New Zealand 1999-2008

Introduction

It would be fair to say that we were going through challenging times when "the book project" was embarked upon. For a start, we were both relocating— literally and figuratively: Gim moved east from New York to Lagos, while Pep headed west from London to Washington D.C. And the rest is fairly complicated.

The project was conceived by Gim one warm April afternoon in 2010, and shared with Pep over a crackling phone line a few weeks later and a continent away. We'd met some months before while working in Nigeria and apparently both needed to channel the mix of emotions that accompany "major change" into something at once focused, creative and bigger than ourselves.

In browsing bookshelves, we had felt a dearth of literature that spoke of the experiences of young women, and believed that it could be heartening, interesting and perhaps even inspiring to offer a glimpse into how some in our generation have thought, felt and dealt with life's "inevitables": men, children, parents, career, self image, faith, dreams.

Knowing that others had likely been there (wherever "that difficult place" might be) gave us, at the time, an inexplicable semblance of reprieve. Thus, we felt that sharing the stories of those around us could provide lessons about the essence of the human condition for others too.

The idea was to bring together women from around the world in their twenties to forties to share parts of their personal journeys. Our premise was simple: while we are unique beings, there are common denominators in the lives of people everywhere—be they on the surface or hidden underneath—which we can take comfort in and draw inspiration from.

Upon starting this (ad)venture, we told everyone we knew about it. That commits you to the project in the public domain so there'll be no backtracking and no procrastination, we were advised. How very true! From conception to fruition, this baby has taken more than a year to deliver. It would probably have taken us longer if friends and colleagues had not prodded us gently along the way, asking, "How's the book coming along?" every now and then. For that, we are indebted!

This book has been a blessing on many fronts. Working on it kept us busy during tough times, but also provided an important source of energy, inspiration and renewal. The project pushed us to juggle schedules and deadlines. It was a reason to be in touch with one another and our authors across continents and time zones. Editing the stories put us for a moment in other women's shoes. Along the way, we've healed.

Our lessons? That life is as random as it is beautiful! That there is much to learn from the people in our midst. And, as many have witnessed, that the spirit is resilient.

Some of the contributors are friends, former classmates and colleagues. Others are friends of friends or people whose paths we have crossed in the course of an ordinary day. In many cases, we have only met "virtually", interacting briefly over the phone, exchanging ideas and edits by email. The fact that more than two dozen women came together to create this, we believe, is part design, part destiny. To the women who put pen to paper, we are deeply grateful for your belief in this project and for your immense trust and generosity in sharing your stories.

We hope that this book will encourage the reader to take heart in others' experiences and to take pride in who you are, regardless of what life is throwing your way at this point in time. When times are trying, take comfort in knowing that you are far from alone—that someone has been there and has come out stronger. And on brighter days, Laugh! Celebrate! Enjoy! We probably don't do it enough.

A final note: We have pledged proceeds from the sale of this book to charitable causes that help women and youth. Thank you for your support.

Pepukaye Bardouille   *Neo Gim Huay*

SUSHI AND TAPAS

EDITORS' NOTE

Little Ghost of Change

Marije is a traveller. For her, every journey is a chance to change, an opportunity to learn and experience a new country. As a human rights activist, she dedicates her time to mobilise, motivate and empower.

Marije's ghost of change was inspired by a drawing on a sidewalk during one of her journeys. She wrote this story at a difficult transition point in her life. Drawing from her childhood and a dose of healthy imagination, she builds perspective on how far she has travelled and more importantly, she harnesses strength for what is to come.

Little Ghost of Change

by Marije Nederveen

She stares back at you or maybe she looks slightly away. Is it a stern, serious or shy look? I'm still not sure. A bow in her hair, a dress which falls to her knees, and shoes like I always wanted, because they make you look like a dancer. A small bag dangles from her left arm. Is she also carrying a small hat?

I found this drawing of a little girl on the side of a pavement in Belgrade, also known as the White City, along the confluence of the Danube and the Sava rivers. I was on my way to a museum, but the guard told me in French that I would need to return the next day; it was closing time.

I never made it back, but the trip was worth it: I ran into her. She looked about four, maybe five years old. Like her, I was taught to look up, something I had trouble with when I was her age. I was shy, preferring to bow my eyes

and promptly blush whenever anyone addressed me. But, I was most certainly not such a perfect dresser. My mum tried her very best—it did not work. I wore similar dresses especially made for me, bows tied in my braided hair and socks pulled up in the morning. All ready for the day.

Somehow, though, the outfit seldom remained in the same shape as evening approached. Socks cheekily slipped down, bows somehow got lost and dresses mysteriously bunched up around my waist, leaving underwear exposed as I stomped my feet through mud and grass. Probably one of the reasons why I was never given those pretty, preppy shoes.

I'm a far cry from that little girl now, but also different from the woman who ran into this image on the pavement just a few months ago.

I was in the White City to take a break, to think and to enjoy a love interest that seemed promising at the time. It started off quite well, but somewhere in the middle we managed to get into an argument. As it goes, I cried, he frowned, then we made up and by the end, contemplated that it could have been different if we had lived closer together, but for now, our story has ended. All in six days.

Still I enjoyed my stay. The beautiful spring weather, the buzz of the city and the random strangers who would talk to me from time to time, one being a man close to his seventies. He said he knew who killed Kennedy and offered himself as the next presidential candidate who would subsequently ensure the replacement of Serbia's cherished republic with a monarchy. Much more fascinating than what I really needed to think about and a fabulous reason to practise my rusty French.

Just before my trip, I had heard that the organisation I was working for was closing down, and then my landlord told me he wanted to sell the apartment I loved. When it rains, it pours. Change had announced itself without my consent, and I wasn't quite sure how to begin dealing with it. Like many women around me, I identified with my job. I really enjoyed the work I did and this one had great benefits—travelling to various countries to meet inspiring people, an opportunity to constantly develop my skills and knowledge, and contribute to something I deeply cared about. It was the job I had been dreaming about since I was a little girl. Maybe not as a five-year-old, but certainly as a fifteen-year-old who desperately wanted to leave the village where she had been exposing her underwear, much to the embarrassment of her mum. The question was, did I take with me any other dreams from that village? Perhaps, when I left the White City, I was little further from where I had begun—I had met the little girl. That was a start.

Back home I posted the picture of the little girl on my social networking page. She drew attention. A friend from Georgia asked where she came from and another lady in Fiji decided to use her as her own profile picture. They simply thought it was moving.

Looking at her again, the text beneath the drawing also fascinates me. Maybe it's the name of the artist that drew her, but the letters aren't really clear. Modern technology doesn't provide any answers: the digit followed by one hundred zeroes gives no Google search hits on the name, the possible date or the numbers—discounting the hits for window shade sizes of course. Seventy-two could be her height, but then what does the other number mean? So whatever the artist's intention, he or she already doesn't want to be credited for it.

And does she represent a real girl? It's like looking at a little ghost. I wondered about it every now and then, but had to leave her again for a while—for one of my travels.

This time to Indonesia. On my day off I found myself on the back of a friend's motorbike. Taking in fumes, sounds and an incredibly diverse group of people humming by on the perpetually congested streets of the vast capital, Jakarta. We were singing African songs I had picked up long ago and he chanted some of his favourite tunes. My friend has no home of his own. He prefers to live in seven different places, combines Sufi wisdom with prayer at a Catholic church and has energy like no other. We had fun hanging out and went to the old part of the city, both enjoying our favourite pastimes: me taking pictures, him making people smile and both of us talking to anyone who would listen. We ended up drinking a coke to face the scorching heat, while a guard of the governor's house we had visited shared a ghost story. A white woman had been murdered over a century ago. I have forgotten the details of her death due to the heat, but the guards reported seeing her at night sometimes. They even laughed as they said she looked like me. I gave them an even bigger grin back as it reminded me of my own little ghost.

Lightning didn't strike then, but a thought did enter my mind: what a wonderful thing it would be to write a story about this woman, or even better, about the little ghost. What a great adventure it would be to find out where she came from, who gave her those watchful eyes that looked straight into the dream I had forgotten about: to write, or better still, to make up stories and share them.

She looked up from under the table. She had been playing there for a while now—waiting to go out, but it was taking more time than she wanted. So long. And it was already one of those very long Sundays. They had been talking first about the weather, then about Papa's work and now about something she didn't understand as they spoke in hushed tones. She looked at the ant that was making its way along the table cloth. It was probably aiming for the sugar that had been spilled when it was added to Aunt Sylvie's tea. Mama was quiet most of the time, but now all of them were silent. She saw how her mother was fumbling with her hands and Papa was tapping his foot. The cat was lying on Aunt Sylvie's lap, being petted feverishly. So much so that he decided to jump off and walk his lazy body out of the kitchen towards the living room.

Freed from the cat, Aunt Sylvie stood up and asked her to come out from under the table. "Shall we go out? I promised you an ice cream right?" She stood up, but felt a bit unsteady on her feet. Her legs had fallen asleep since she had been sitting in the same position for so long. "Are you OK?" Aunt Sylvie asked. She nodded. "We will go to the ice cream parlour and buy you a treat," Aunt Sylvie said.

This awkward conversation seemed directed more towards Mama than to her, she thought. Her mother's face was a bit strange when she smiled at her and said: "Be careful of your dress." "She's a big girl, she will be fine Anna," her aunt replied on her behalf, giving a comforting glance.

The parlour was only a few blocks away and she ran ahead enjoying the fresh air after the some-what stuffy kitchen. Her new shoes didn't run that easily, but she felt like a dancer wearing them. She held her bag and hat tight, afraid that she might lose them. The parlour was busy and much as craned her neck, she could not see the different kinds of milky delights on offer until it was their turn. Her aunt ordered her favourites—chocolate, vanilla and strawberry. Normally she wouldn't get three scoops, but Aunt Sylvie said it was a day for a little extra.

After the ice cream, they walked to the playground, but she only played on the swings. The slide might make her dress dirty and Mama would be really upset. On a usual day, she would have wanted to stay longer, but now she just wanted to go back home. She asked Aunt Sylvie, who looked at her watch and sighed, "Yes, I think we can go back now."

She entered the kitchen. Her mother was at the same position at the table. "Mama, where's Papa?" Aunt Sylvie spoke before her mother did. "Your father will stay with your uncle and me for a while until he finds a new home. Don't worry though, you will see him soon." She dropped her hat and bag. Her mother started to cry.

There's a picture of me, also in black and white, that I found again when I was moving into my new home. I'm about four years old, holding the hand of a friend. One sock is up, the other down, my braids are lit up by the sunlight from behind and my bangs all over the place. I'm wearing an overcoat which grazes my knees and look quite happily into the camera. That little girl told stories, made up stories, and would share them with anyone that would listen.

I hope there are many more to come.

• • •

Marije Nederveen is a sociologist with a passion for human rights. Through her work she has had the opportunity to travel extensively in Asia and Africa. After working for a while for a sustainable development organisation in South Africa, she is back in her home country, the Netherlands, focusing on human rights issues. Marije enjoys meeting and working with people who dedicate their time to mobilising, motivating and empowering others, and captures her experiences in short stories, poetry, performances and pictures.

EDITORS' NOTE

On the Road to Oman

This is a story about a friendship and a romantic encounter. In the randomness of events, two persons' paths cross and later separate, leaving only memories to be relished as the years pass. However, just because separations can be painful does not mean we should shy away from a union in the first place. Similarly, just because loving or being loved can be empowering does not mean we should cling on and never let go. Indeed, it is the unexpected complexity of human interactions that makes life exciting and brings out the best of us.

Sarah's story reminds us to let life flow—to experience the moment as is and to allow memories, be they wonderful or sad, to simply coalesce because they are what make us who we are.

On the Road to Oman

by Sarah de Freitas

It was yet another road trip with my good friend... a good friend who always pops up at the "introns" or spaghetti-tangled moments of my life, such as when I went searching for my dad at age nineteen. Looking back, my friend has always been there, missing only the moments that have been edited out as unimportant on the cutting room floor of my memory.

I like my friend so much that even the thought of him makes me smile. Years ago he told me he was learning to fly. I hate flying and during turbulence would close my eyes and imagine that he was sitting in the cockpit with a big grin on his face, steering the plane. Even after he told me he'd given up flying because he wasn't any good at it, I still used that image of him to derive comfort.

I was on the road trip escaping some of my own

turbulence after a three year relationship had crashed unexpectedly. The unexpected bit included a curt email and the man in question running off to the ends of the earth (on a trip to the Amazon), with his mother as a replacement companion (hmm).

Looking back, I was worn down because life had not been easy for a while. A year of feeling the relationship slip away, despite my efforts, had taken its toll. I was a believer in the philosophy of "working harder" so this break-up left me devastated. Wise clichés such as "it just wasn't meant to be" and "when one door closes, another opens" are difficult to swallow when in free fall.

A broken heart is an extraordinary thing and I was baffled by how destroyed I felt. How could this be worse than the loss of a loved relative? Fortunately I had switched from a high pressure medical job to a less demanding research job and, for a time, could be dispassionate at work without it being detrimental or even noticeable. "Time out" for emotional flailing about prevented the stain of bitterness and lost optimism from becoming permanent. "Give sorrow words. The grief that does not speak whispers the o'er-fraught heart, and bids it break" (Shakespeare).

In a jeep heading from Dubai to Oman with my friend, I was very much in the emotional flailing about stage. I was giving sorrow far too much air time, and my poor friend ended up listening to this and that about my ex for seven days. He told me many times as we bumped along that dusty road what a great guy my ex sounded like, which I found really irritating, though obviously I'd liked my ex for a reason!

To be fair, my ex had never done anything bad, apart from allowing me to think that we would be together forever, even after he'd stopped feeling it, thus wasting my time (fertility) but not his own. My female friends were compassionate but much of that compassion followed a "men are mean" format, which had its place in the grief cycle (anger) but at some point I needed to leave that loop, recalibrate and tune it all out.

I still had one foot in the men-are-mean camp on this trip, which my friend approached with amusement. Let me give you an example of one of our many "women think men are mean but men think women are even meaner" conversations. In this instance we were talking about why some husbands cheat on their wives soon after the birth of a first child:

Me: *It's terrible... and just because that woman is not so sexy and starts pampering the baby instead of her brat of a husband he runs off with someone who's got time to* *dress up and flatters his ego more.*

Friend: *But hang on a minute what if that woman never really loved the guy and just married him for the money, baby and security (cheque book with sperm scenario). What if once the baby's born she turns mean and lets herself go as she's already got all that she ever wanted from the relationship and he realises the whole thing was a sham...*

Makes you think, I suppose.

My friend and I drove around for about a week. The stars by the sea at night in Oman are bright enough to lift the heaviest of hearts. It was deeply nourishing to break from normal worldly ties to talk about sadness but also about life.

We went back to Dubai for a couple of days, and on the day of my flight to London he announced feelings for me. Given my droning on about my ex during the week, it took me by surprise. I had been too preoccupied to observe my attentive listener. I had not even reached the "first cut is the deepest" stage (Cat Stevens) when one can just about give scraps of one's heart to someone new. Despite a wrong turn on the road to the airport, I made the flight. I'm sorry to say it but I really needed to make that flight. I could not give what was deserved.

I thought intensely on the plane, looking back at everything we'd talked about. It sounded different knowing how it must have made the listener feel and also trying to figure out what the future now held. I landed feeling more optimistic and it was not long before I was on a plane again to see him, perhaps still a bit before the bandages should have come off. We did not work out. Not in a bad way. The strength of the friendship barely flickered and we are always able to be happy for each other.

Thinking about my friend still makes me smile but I'm in love with somebody new and so is he.

• • •

Sarah de Freitas' heritage is Portuguese, but she was born and raised in England. She is a doctor, and lives in London.

EDITORS' NOTE

I'm Fat

Some time ago, I asked the husband-to-be of a good friend, "What do you love most about her?" He replied unequivocally, "Her confidence." This was my first revelation that self-assuredness in a woman could be beautiful and a powerful source of attraction to men.

How often do we allow advertisements to bombard us with lofty promises of beauty enhancing treatments? How many hours do we spend in front of the mirror wistfully thinking of all the changes we want to make to our bodies?

Chè's story flies in the face of these "image destroyers" and "soul depleters". It is a tale of coming of age—the winding road of becoming comfortable with who we are, and learning to love ourselves. We are reminded that, in whatever shape or form, we are part of nature. There is beauty in nature. And there is beauty in being natural.

I'm Fat

by Chè Monique Young

I'm fat. I have been for as long as I can remember. I'm not sure how I feel about that. Fat is a very loaded word and fat is what I am. Fat is not like ugly. Fat is not an annoying voice. Fat isn't ditzy or being a bitch. Those things, while people may not like them, are accepted as permanent characteristics of a person. Being fat, however, comes with the expectation that you are unhappy and trying hard to get rid of it. But I'm tired of being unhappy with half of my physical self and wishing it away.

Perhaps to make sense of how this all began, I treat the story of my fat like it's folklore or a fairy tale.

Once upon a time there was a beautiful girl name Donna. She was tall, skinny and athletic. She went to a private school and preferred to wear boys' blazers because her limbs were so long. She finished high school when afros were fashionable and a huge round 'fro haloed her head in her senior year photo. Donna went off to college and met a dangerous and exciting man named Tim. Donna and Tim wed in 1980. They had a spectacular ceremony—people still talk about it thirty years later.

Five years after they married, Donna became pregnant. Everyone was excited. This baby was to be the first grandchild on both sides of the family. In fact, so many people were eagerly anticipating the new arrival that Donna was given at least four baby showers.

At last the baby was born, Chè Robyn-Monique Young. Chè was a small baby even by 1980s standards, weighing in at six pounds ten ounces. She was too small for the homecoming outfit that Donna had carefully picked out. Stockings hung off her legs making her look like a tiny bird.

Donna was so concerned about how little her baby was that she weighed Chè daily on a kitchen scale. She also prayed that the baby would become plump. Miracle of miracles, Chè packed on the pounds. In fact, by the time she was a toddler, her father had taken to calling her "bruiser".

Poor Donna was still not happy. While she longed for a chubby baby, she did not want a fat child, especially not a fat daughter. There was nothing Donna could do; she had prayed for her baby to gain weight and that's precisely what had happened. Donna tried everything to undo her prayer so that this girl, who by now was no longer so little, could be as beautiful and skinny as her mother. While Chè was in elementary school, Donna put her on numerous diets including the "Cabbage Soup Diet" and "Fit For Life". Donna would send Chè to school with lunch boxes packed with breadless sandwiches: lettuce wrapped around lunch meat, and a pickle. On occasion, lunch would consist entirely of a quarter of a watermelon. The kids at school found Chè's meals quite peculiar. While other kids were busy with extracurricular activities, Chè was at home following the routine of an aerobics video. Over time, Donna partook in these slimming plans as well. Donna was never particularly fat, but she was not happy with the way her body was changing; a once tiny waistline was starting to succumb to several pregnancies and, frankly, to life itself. She was now trying to drop between five and thirty pounds at any given point. When Donna was pregnant with her third child, nine-year-old Chè weighed more than she did. After Donna gave birth, she and Chè joined Weight Watchers together.

As Chè got older, Donna resorted to bribery, promising her beautiful leather and fur coats if she could just drop the pounds. But that didn't work. She then told Chè that boys and, later, men would be more interested in her if she were thin. But Chè never slimmed. Her weight would always be the elephant in the room for those two. They couldn't break bread, go shopping or plan a family activity without the weight issue coming up.

I wish I could tell the story of my fat, of my weight, of my insecurities without discussing my mother. She isn't fat. She isn't me. It is true that, somehow very early in my life, possibly from the very day I was born, when she decided I was too small and something had to be done about that, my mother rooted herself deeply in the prospect of creating the perfect physique for me. Yet, there's more to my fat than my mother and that's what I would like to talk about.

I've always been a little odd. Smart, assertive and independent, I never quite fit in anywhere, not at any time in my life. I generally attributed this to being fat, rather than to my, shall we call it, quirky personality. I was slower in speed than other kids, bad at sports and boys didn't like me.

Not being a fashionista herself, my mother dressed me

in men's pants that were too small and put me in oversized men's T-shirts. Through elementary and middle school I would have to lie flat on my back to squeeze into a pair of jeans, and then sit uncomfortably through class all day with my legs sandwiched like a couple of sardines in that "one-size-too-small" outfit. If ever there were a special event and I needed to dress up for it, invariably I'd end up resembling a grandma.

By middle school, I'd accepted that boys would never like me. I was fat, black and ugly. I was the fat friend. In fact, throughout middle school, high school and college, if I were attending a co-ed event, I understood clearly that the boys would be interested in all my friends, but never in me.

In gym class in the seventh grade, Steven teased me for having hairy legs so I decided to exclusively wear trousers. Later that summer, Alex, an older boy on whom I had a major crush, joked about the fat lumps on my upper arms that looked like muscles. From then on I never wore tank tops. I endured one or two very hot summers of long jeans and big shirts before I had my first epiphany. You can't hide fat. It wouldn't matter if I wore a burqa or a bikini, I would still look fat.

Naked Chè was born. I started wearing clothes that were less oppressive. I found that the fewer clothes I wore, the more comfortable I was. I was making quite a bit of money babysitting at this point and spent the overwhelming majority of it on clothing and Frappacinos. From ages fourteen to twenty-three, I dressed like a bit of a skank. I wasn't fond of wearing bras, despite having size 40DD breasts, because they weren't comfortable. Comfort and cuteness were now the driving factors in my choice of attire. Because I was always flitting about in a state of partial nudity, people assumed that I was really comfortable in my own skin. The truth is, like everyone else, sometimes I was, and sometimes I just wasn't.

What really helped me to become comfortable in my own skin was the mirror. Through high school I, like many adolescents, would spend hours staring at myself. I was constantly evaluating and reevaluating the image that stared back at me. In the process I became desensitised to my size and began to see beyond it.

The more I looked at "the fat", the less it disgusted me. The more innocuous it became. I realised it wasn't ugly.

I also began to take note of the fact that fat feels good. It is soft and warm. The kids I babysat loved for me to hold and hug them. I guess that meant that fat could be comforting.

Through looking at myself, touching myself and realising that self-hatred is not productive, I began to love who I am.

This was not a magical development. Nobody sneakily sprinkled fairy dust while I slept, allowing me to somehow awake as the spokeswoman for happy, fat girls. Instead, it was a process of sorts. Over time, I began to develop certain core beliefs about myself and the world. One is that it's OK to be fat and if someone has a problem with fat, that's their problem not mine. Another is that I'm incredibly sexy. Sexy, I've learned over the years, is quite a super power.

When I was about sixteen or seventeen, I read about Big Burlesque in San Francisco—an entire troupe of fat ladies who were sexy as hell and embraced it. These women strutted their stuff half-naked but in surprisingly tasteful outfits, like Parisien damsels in feathers and ruffles at the Moulin Rouge in days gone by. They used their body not just to entertain men, but to tell a story for which the opening line was: "You come here to look at me because I am the essence of woman; because I am beautiful."

I dreamed of running away and joining them, but when I was twenty-one, I realised I didn't have to go very far. I discovered the DC Gurly Show, a local burlesque troupe made up of women of all body types, age, sexual orientation and gender identity. I decided that I liked this inclusivity even more than I liked the idea of Big Burlesque. Where Big Burlesque says that fat women are sexy, the DC Gurly

Show says that all people are sexy. There's no othering or qualifying involved.

I joined the troupe in 2007 and loved having an outlet to be openly sexual and overtly sensual without anyone expecting me to first apologise for being fat. And the funny thing is that people do not only see past the weight, they love it.

Right now, I am one of the more confident people I know. I want to just say "I'm fat, so what"? And, in many ways, that's what I do. I don't let being fat hold me back or stop me from living life to the fullest. But fat, like I said earlier, is still complicated.

While I can accept my fat from a beauty and self esteem perspective, a lot of the world doesn't. Being fat limits my dating options, clothing options, job options. It affects my fertility and chances of having a healthy pregnancy, and living a long life. It also increases my risks of developing heart disease, diabetes, cancer and other major illnesses. So, to say that it's OK to be fat or that I'm not going to make any effort to lose weight seems like I'm giving up on myself.

How can I intelligently accept that?

I've been on and off diets my whole life and I'm tired of it. I can't look you in the eye and promise to start eating healthier and exercising for my wellbeing. See, when I do those things, I'm not thinking about lower blood pressure or higher energy levels. I'm really thinking about smaller pants sizes and more men finding me attractive.

In fact, I'm currently trying to convince myself to lose eighty pounds by Halloween so I can dress up as Beyoncé.

But, hopefully as I continue to mature I'll find a contented place and make decisions driven more by what makes me healthy. Who knows what the future holds. Right now I'm fat. I'm confident. I'm sexy. I'm conflicted. I'm imperfect. I'm at risk for all sorts of problems. I'm happy. I'm human.

• • •

Chè Monique Young was raised and resides in Virginia, USA. She holds a Bachelor's Degree in Women's Studies from Temple University and is a massage therapist, belly dancer and burlesque performer. Chè is currently planning workshops to help women tap into their own "sexy" and let go of unnecessary baggage related to body image.

EDITORS' NOTE

The Tea Lady in the Boardroom

It is not often that one is so inspired by a young colleague. When it does happen, one pauses to reflect upon the beauty of life, then doubles up on pace to make up for time lost in experiencing its richness.

Zipho's life reads like an opera—growing up in the new nation of South Africa, in an environment of poverty and sickness, in a world where both her skin colour and gender have been and, in some instances, still are being discriminated against. She has faced more challenges than some women twice her age, yet Zipho has triumphed over them. She reminds me of fresh buds in spring, bursting with hope, resilience and energy after a savage winter. She is the future that the end of apartheid had hoped for and a fountain of strength from which we can all draw.

The Tea Lady
in the Boardroom

by Zipho Sikhakhane

Here I am sitting at a long oval table, which looks exactly like the ones I have seen on television. Black leather seats, flowers and paintings all around the room. I am clicking away at the back of my pen, wearing a fancy black suit like everyone else. There is a side table with teacups, saucers and spoons placed neatly next to a pile of biscuits. I have imagined this day for many years now, the very moment when I finally feel like I have made it! Today marks my first boardroom meeting.

When the meeting commences, my mother walks in wearing a black and white apron and she starts serving tea around the table. It is customary in African culture that I see every Black Woman as my mother and every Black Man as my father. By instinct I want to get up and help her serve the tea. After all, I was raised to be a good servant. My brain quickly reminds me that I should not do that in a board meeting. Rather, I should continue with the discussions at hand and ignore what is happening in the background. I pretend to concentrate, although the urge to assist constantly nags me, as my mother serves one cup after another. My turn for tea arrives and all I do is smile and say thank you.

The sound of the shutting door upon her exit brings sadness to my eyes since I have just betrayed my own cultural norms. A glance across the room makes me realise that no one else here can relate to this—I am the only black woman present! Everyone else is white, male and decades older than I am. In contrast, they look comfortable, so much at ease, as if they have been doing this for centuries! Big English words tumble out from one mouth to another, as page by page the discussion document is presented. I turn into a mute and begin praying for the earth to swallow me up, especially now as the others have started sneaking glimpses in my direction! Perhaps I am not the only one feeling uneasy with my presence.

The big question of how I landed myself in this exclusive boardroom starts to linger in my head. My brain reminds me: it is just the outcome of a little girl's dream to make it big in business against all the odds! This is the very room I have spent all my life hoping to get into. Even today, in the New South Africa, when a girl child is raised well in the poor black community, her future is defined as a wife, a house cleaner or a tea lady. The ambitious ones become teachers or nurses. None of these really appealed to me because I was a "societal non-conformer"—a term I invented to describe an innate need not to let my future be defined by the views of other human beings. I inevitably aimed for the businesswoman route because this would get me a ticket into the exclusive boardroom I had dreamt about. I ignored the words of discouragement and numerous giggles received when I shared this dream with others. I wanted to beat the odds and this meant I needed to deviate from seeing the future in South Africa as a divided field comprised of black careers and white careers.

I see myself as the empty vessel that makes the loudest noise. Unlike the vessel though, when it came to the crunch, I would make sure my vessel was full and showed no signs of inadequacy. Starting with my grades in school, I tried to push them to perfection. This involved ensuring that there were matches and candles on standby, given that power outages were quite common when I tried to study late into the night. I kept this up all the way through to university and even resorted to sitting in cold rooms in the middle of the night just so I could fight the urge to fall asleep. Eventually my academic record was good enough for me to walk the talk, but somehow I needed to learn how to talk the talk in the proper way.

Her name was Brooke Logan, a beautiful blonde character in the American soap opera *The Bold and the Beautiful*. Lines uttered with elegance, her vocabulary always contained some strange English word that I had never heard before. The perfect role model to mimic. Every day at 6pm I would get my dictionary, turn on the television and glue myself to the screen for the next half hour. The dictionary eventually fell to bits because I had flicked through it in many rushed moments to interpret every new word Brooke had uttered. Occasionally, I would go into momentary distress when words such as "bouquet" or "rendezvous" were used, since their pronunciations are nothing close to how they are spelt!

Eventually I could walk and talk right, but somehow I needed evidence of my worthiness to be in that dimly lit meeting room that would define my success.

In between my school lectures, I completed every part time job that would have me. That way I would have a stream of people ready to vouch for my proficiency should the need arise. I knew I had somewhat surpassed this goal when one interviewer looked at me in shock and said, "So you are Superwoman?" She was serious and not the first to use this term. I had been a receptionist, tutor, shopkeeper, entertainer, speaker, writer, auditor, all in one year—you name it, I had done it.

I eventually believed I was ready to try out the boardroom and chose a career that granted me an entry ticket. Management consulting presented me with the key to enter. The only trick was that I had to work hard so that my manager would reward me with the privilege of joining the client's management team in the boardroom. That moment had finally arrived.

South Africa is no longer a divided country—my attendance in this meeting is evidence that it is possible for minorities to cross the line. My heart is supposed to be doing a little dance in celebration given this is what I have long coveted. Instead I feel like an alien—not the one with three eyes, but rather a different sex altogether—with thick lips, coarse hair and a somewhat burned complexion. An alien who deserted her roots by not getting on her knees and serving everyone tea in the respectable fashion that her own mother had taught her. My culture commands that I never sit on a chair if any man is around—it is a sign of disrespect. Yet here I am sitting at the same table with males and no one thought to bring a floor mat for me to sit on in the corner. Business etiquette commands that I look people in the eye when I speak to them, else I will be mistrusted or construed as having low self-confidence. My culture scorns any woman who looks an elderly person in the eye, especially when addressing them. The rules are simple: lower your head, join your hands together, and speak quietly—not in this loud commanding voice that I am expected to project in the room, certainly not with my hands above the table, and perhaps even waving them around while I speak to assert a point. I should be giving precedence to the opinions of my superiors, not challenging discussion points that I disagree with.

While everyone else was busy tackling the business issue at hand, I was distracted with my own internal battles—fighting to prevent my culture from creeping into the boardroom setting, for fear that I may never ever be invited to attend these meetings again. At the same time I caution my instincts not to erase the behaviours which my family and community have taught me—especially since I need to exercise these when I get home. I am reminded that at home the business suit comes off and the pants will be replaced with a long, respectable skirt. I will be acting in the traditions of any well-raised Zulu woman. I will receive my orders for the day and respectively oblige without showing any signs of restraint.

It would be a waste if I choose to discard my culture and its teachings from here onwards; after all who ever said being different was something to be ashamed of? Perhaps embracing some elements of my culture may just help me last longer than the typical person in this boardroom world.

For one, meetings always reach a juncture where people start being harsh as they linger and argue about one discussion point. I know I will never be caught in the heat of these arguments, as being humble and maintaining composure is part of my cultural blueprint. I am scarcely given occasion to express an opinion in my culture, so whenever I get the chance I use it right. The fact that at home I am on my knees, to give respect to whoever is in the room, means I am not afraid to push aside my perspective and consider the views of others. Because my eye is no regular playing field, my big idea or final price can never be predicted by my business associates until I verbalise it. That big idea presented by an elegant black woman can never really be forgotten—my soft tone and select vocabulary means that no one else can sell it like I can. I am not one of the guys in the room.

I will not squirm when times get tough; after all, I have seen many a chicken, sheep and cow slain in front of my naked eyes, and had barely flinched at the sight. My grandmother taught me that a woman should never shy away from doing chores all day and every day—so the day will likely never come when I am worn out from yet another late night at the office. When the business makes a profit, it is not my own needs and wants that I think of. Instead, I imagine how I can invest it back into the community. After all, I am already used to spreading my pay cheque among at least fifteen relatives.

Everyone gets up and starts shaking hands and exchanging business cards—the meeting is over. My manager whispers in my ear that I need to quickly follow through on some queries that had arisen during the discussion. I nod, even though I had heard none of these queries. My thoughts had been lost in the puzzle of a divided life. The tea lady walks back in to collect the cups and realises that I had stayed behind to help pack everything away. She flashes a smile of pride that could only mean one thing, "I wish she were my daughter."

We eventually leave the boardroom together and, frankly, I still do not know which role I was destined to play in that room: the tea lady or the businesswoman.

Dadewethu Ntombazane Mfazi Nkosikazi, Lalela!
[English: My Lady, Woman, Wife, Listen!]

She screams in pain
Everyone smiles
And no one sees her pain
Let's rejoice, the baby is born!

The bitch of the town, she is called

Family wrecker, her middle name

The married lover was drawn to her charm

'tis not his fault

The woman takes all the blame.

Scars and memory she must bear

Yes, the perpetrator must be punished

Let's discuss HIS sentence!

What of the pain of the rape victim

> The punching bag
>
> The kitchen slave
>
> The toilet cleaner

Oh gosh, what of the mere rib of Adam?

Who are we? "Women"?

Is there more to us than just

Breasts, looks, hair, curves and make up?

Do we exist just to WOO men.

Or are we women because we are

> Mothers of the nations
>
> Sisters of the universe
>
> Daughters of fallen leaders

Or maybe, just maybe

We are the...

... shush, listen, hear for I will explain.

Women are
Symbols of happiness
New life just when humanity thought all was over
Oh yes, we breed sunshine on those cold days
That string of masculinity, just when all men gave up.
We are like those mere seeds
That emerge into trees
And bring out beautiful fruits!

Quite vulnerable on the outside
Yes we admit
But strong, firm, mighty on the inside!
How else could we have mothered all the leaders
of this world?
How else could we still stand and celebrate after
so many struggles?!

"Pass laws" we protested
And many more we shall change
Ah yes, we can make much change
Because, when placed together
We are like dynamite!

The roads are still far
The gaps in the system still exist
But we will strive

Ah yes we will

For we are the rainbow to this world of thunderstorms.

Uma uke wathinta umfazi

Wathi ukum' nyakazisa nje

Uzobe uthinte imbokodo!

[English: If you ever touch a woman

Even a slight nudge,

You have struck a rock!]

• • •

Zipho Sikhakhane was born and raised in the new South Africa. She dreams big dreams and yet remains grounded in how she relates to friends and family. Zipho has a passion for transforming organisations in Africa using the qualities that make her different. She grew up hand to mouth and had to persevere to make it through the system by starting up multiple small business ventures to support her living expenses. She obtained a business degree at the University of Cape Town and will be completing her MBA at Stanford Graduate Business School in 2014. She hopes to inspire other young women to beat the odds in their lives, believing that anything is possible and striving to make this an everyday reality.

EDITORS' NOTE

Precious

"Troubled by men, wrecked by love. Manage your emotions so you don't walk the path that has devastated many a woman before you," an elderly woman advises. We are emotional creatures—that makes us human. So how do we prevent emotions from overwhelming us and pushing us into a downward spiral of despair? This is a heart-wrenching story about a journey through a minefield of men and broken hearts before crossing onto the path of love and God. When one takes pain and manifests it into goodness, we can believe that there is a bigger plan and a larger force at play. Pain becomes a privilege bestowed upon us to be turned into something noble.

At the heart of Suzie's story is the message that love heals, that we are valuable and worthy of loving ourselves. And, when we do, our capacity to love others becomes infinite.

Precious

by Suzie Walker

As a little girl, I dreamed of being rescued. I dreamed that someone would come along and gently release the grip of a dark secret that I had held on to very tightly for a long time. I would be protected and the secret would be taken far, far away. My story is about being rescued, being fully restored and being made whole again. It's about experiencing some difficult things in life and, for too long, thinking that "It doesn't matter", that "This is just life!" There are plenty of people who will tell you so. Enough people that you start to believe that whatever you feel doesn't really matter, and also that you don't really matter—your opinions, your values, your beliefs—none of these things matter. For too long I settled in the belief that life throws things at you mercilessly and all you can do is to try your best to overcome them and soldier on.

No longer.

Each excruciating event is relevant. These things impact what we do next in a deeper and heavier way, distracting and muddying the senses, gnawing away at the soul in ways that appear impossible to heal. Whatever source we draw upon for the strength to recover, we must never ignore pain.

Despite my parents not being Christians, they chose to send me to Anglican boarding schools from the age of seven. They had hoped that the schools would provide me with a good moral foundation. But what developed went beyond that. I started to believe that God existed and that I wanted to be part of his family. This was met with mild disapproval from my parents and a belief that it was just a phase that I would grow out of, like having an imaginary friend.

At my secondary school, my best friend's dad was an army chaplin and her family lived their lives in a way that showed me how I could get to know God more deeply. I would pray with them and visit their lively church gatherings that were very different from the quiet and reserved Anglican services that I was used to attending. She and I were also members of a Christian youth group. It was with this youth group that I went along to a particularly inspiring talk by students from

Cambridge University about the healing power of Jesus. Afterwards, while sitting in the corner of a dark, smoky pub, surrounded by fellow underage drinkers, I suddenly felt able to confide in one of the university students and tell her a secret that I had been carrying for eight years and never shared with anyone else. I asked her to pray for me. That night was the beginning of a long journey of healing.

It started with having to gather up enough courage to ask my sister if our older brother (seven years my senior, nine years her senior) had ever touched her or made her do things that she didn't want to do. I needed to ask her these questions for two reasons. Firstly, if he had, I would do what I could to help her, and secondly, because on a fateful day eight years earlier when I had been bold enough to tell my brother, "I don't want to do this anymore," he had asked me, "But what am I supposed to do now?" Desperate for him to leave me alone, I blurted out, "Go to my little sister." Awful. He protested that she was too young, and I remember thinking, "Strange, since she is the age that I was when you first started on me."

My little sister smirked at me in embarrassment (I wanted to slap her). "No, he has never touched me," she said. Such a sense of relief. The guilt of volunteering her had haunted me.

I've always maintained that the acts themselves, although horribly unpleasant and bewildering, have had less impact on me than the carrying of the ugly secret itself. But as I write this, I find myself realising that it's not really the case. Both have shaped the way in which I have behaved and valued myself. I had thought that it didn't really matter if bad stuff happened to me physically or mentally and had accepted it—that is just life, right? You just have to march on.

But crappy decisions and choices built on damaging things that happen have a way of piling on top of each other, and the foundations of your life start rotting under the layers of detritus that mount up.

When I was thirteen, I was teased by my best friend for begging a boy, whom I had been kissing in the bushes outside a school disco, not to undo the belt of my trousers (the boy was a friend of her brother's, which is how she'd found out). After that, I decided that I was going to take control. I wasn't going to be scared of sex. I was going to instigate it. I lost my virginity to a boy whose surname I did not know, in a four poster bed in a castle in Germany. Classy, I thought. I was fourteen. I proceeded to sleep with eight others (two of them brothers) until, at the age of twenty, I met the man whom I realised was going to rescue me from this life of promiscuity.

Having severed contact with my best friend and her family three years before, after a major fall out, precipitated by an argument over a boy, I had struggled with my relationship with God and had decided to make my own way in life. And, as if to prove that I didn't need God, here was my new saviour. I fell madly in love with him. I felt completed by him. He made me feel so loved and cherished, so restored. He knew everything about me and accepted me. He was handsome and strong, intelligent, quick-witted and adored by my family. We had the perfect life mapped out ahead of us—everything I'd ever dreamed of.

Then something happened that threw us off course. Our fairy tale wedding was only five months away when I discovered that I was pregnant. I was twenty-two. The perfect life I wanted so badly was suddenly under threat. Being pregnant was yet another thing that I couldn't bear telling my parents. The stupidity and irresponsibility of it all knocked me out totally. Had I not gone through enough? Was I going to be denied this chance of a perfect life? Something I didn't want happening was happening to me. I considered what I could do, faced with this thing beyond my control, and looked to my past for an answer.

What was revealed to me was that I should muster enough courage to stop it. In the same way that I had said no to my brother, I could say no to this. My fiancé also didn't want to start a family so early, and I was desperate to make him happy. I drowned out the voices of doubt, convincing myself that terminating the pregnancy would put my life back on track and that any deeper feelings I had—a yearning for the baby that was growing inside me, the preciousness of its life—were not worthy of any further consideration. It doesn't matter, I convinced myself. It's just a foetus, medically speaking. This is just another hurdle you need to cross before you can have your wonderful life with this amazing man.

Sadly things didn't quite turn out that way. Our marriage started with me sinking into a depression after the abortion, from which my husband shrunk away, preferring to sweep the issue under the carpet. I desperately needed to talk about how I felt. I realise now that the shame and guilt that he felt prevented him from being able to talk about it. Both of us were working long hours, he was often away on business during the week. We busied ourselves doing up a two bedroom flat and sold it less than a year later to move up the property ladder. Next we bought a five bedroom house with a garden and started to renovate that. We went on expensive holidays abroad, hosted popular parties and pretended to be happy. After all, we had everything, didn't we?

I longed to have a baby but he kept saying that we couldn't afford to. He had always drunk a lot, particularly with his university friends, but while they started settling down and drinking less, he continued to drink as much as he did in his student days. His behaviour became erratic and controlling. He stopped wanting to have sex. Gradually, we became two separate individuals living under the same roof. Nothing I tried pulled him back to me. Eventually I decided to accept the marriage for what it was and stopped trying to change it. It was at that point that he conceded and offered me something he knew that I wanted. "Let's start a family!" he announced. My response surprised him, "There's no way that I want to bring a baby into this relationship, the way it is." I wanted to be a mother but I also desperately needed a good husband and father for my children. "In any case," I snidely pointed out, "you'd have to sleep with me to make that happen." "It only takes once," he retorted. My heart shrivelled and, not for the first time, I felt utterly alone.

He left me three months later. We had the most frank conversation in two years on the day that he left. I couldn't understand why he was leaving just as we'd manage to connect again. But I knew he'd only managed to be so open because he had decided to leave. I was devastated.

I went into work the following Monday and people asked, "Nice weekend?" "Not great," I replied. "My husband left me." It was surreal.

A couple of months later, I went to Turkey for a holiday, choosing a tour operator who specialised in boutique hotels located in unspoiled, rural parts of the country. It was during that trip that I remembered how I had once wanted to work in the tourism industry. I decided to apply for a job in Turkey with that same holiday company. I got the position and spent two years looking after holiday-makers in a beautiful remote spot on the southwest coast. I met a Turkish guy who became my boyfriend. I felt alive and happy and in the moment. Looking to the future though, things didn't feel quite right. My new boyfriend made it clear that if we were ever to get married, I would have to convert to Islam.

It got me thinking, "What would I be converting from?" I realised that it would involve me renouncing Christianity and this threw up all sorts of questions. If I felt that I had to renounce Jesus, then surely it meant that I still believed that He existed, and if He existed, could I really renounce Him? Even without being able to answer those questions at that time, I left my boyfriend after the tourist season ended and returned to the UK. I settled back into the flat that I had bought after the divorce.

One day, while lamenting about my life with a friend—
the lack of fulfilment I felt and how, despite doing all kinds
of things that I thought would fill the emptiness, I was
still left wondering what it was all about—she suggested
that I do The Alpha Course, a ten-week programme run by
many churches around the world, that helped explore the
meaning of life. I agreed, thinking that it would help me
answer the questions that had arisen in Turkey.

Three weeks into the course, I found myself writing
in my notes: "My determination to find God is currently
matched by my determination to resist Him." Eventually I
realised that I was having to try harder and harder to ignore
Jesus, which could only mean that he did exist, he did die
for me, he did save me and he loved me and longed to have
me back in His family. I realised that I wanted to be fully
restored by the power of his forgiveness, mercy and grace
and I wanted to discover my true potential in this world—
one unhampered by the mistakes I had already made.

Over the years, I've seen five therapists, each with
varying degrees of success, but all contributing in some
way to where I find myself today. But it's the knowledge
of God's unwavering love and goodness that sustains me
constantly. He reminds me that I'm precious, so much
so that he died for me. I know that he has a plan for me
and is guiding me along the path ahead. I've discovered

a deep sense of joy which sustains me through periods of unhappiness because I know that he loves me and wants the best for me. I've found perfection that is not possible to find in any human.

As I reflect, I see that I was looking for a Jesus-like perfection in my ex-husband—clearly a bit of a high order! I had really begun to wonder if I was beyond rescue, but it's only through Jesus that I've been renewed, learnt how to forgive, been forgiven, washed clean and restored to be "me" personified. I am free to mourn my childhood, mourn my baby, mourn my marriage. Perhaps one of the most challenging things that I've faced is realising that part of God's plan to heal me would involve waiting until I'm married to have sex again. But since the tally has reached a dizzy nineteen men, I think that this is probably wise. I miss sex—it's a whole different language, the touching, the tasting, the intimacy, the excitement, the abandonment—I love it! But I feel precious now and I feel that my body is a gift that I have to offer my husband. Extraordinary really when you think of the appalling treatment it's received.

In spite of this newfound meaning, I am still single. But where that would have previously meant that I would be sleeping around, trying to find love, and getting hurt along the way, I fall back on my faith and trust that the right man is lined up for me and will come along when the time is right.

That's not to say that I don't cry out to God asking him to please, please hurry up and reveal that man to me. I've tried internet dating, had friends set me up on dates, all while working in a male-dominated environment, to no avail. However the difference is that I am no longer at the mercy of men. I do not need them to make me feel that I am worthy of being loved. I do not need them to reveal how my life will play out. I am at ease with not really knowing what's in store for me because life is an amazing adventure when you know in your heart that you are protected, you are worthy, you are precious, and you are always loved.

There's great liberty in knowing that each day I'm called to transform myself in this knowledge.

I've found a meaning to life, a purpose to serve and to pursue a deeper understanding of my loving God. Right now, that entails doing my part in trying to alleviate poverty; listening, training, encouraging and facilitating opportunities for people in my local community to transform their lives. My hope is that one day it will also entail being a wife and a mother.

I met a man last week. He complimented me on my toes. They were painted with shiny red polish. He loves the Lord and makes my heart flutter...

• • •

Suzie Walker was born and raised in England. She has lived and worked in Belgium, USA, Turkey, Croatia and more recently, Africa. She enjoys horse riding and is easily drawn to doing anything adventurous. God, family, friends and animals play a large part in her life.

EDITORS' NOTE

Suddenly, Without a Map

This is the longest and one of the most emotive stories in the collection. We made a conscious decision not to edit it for length so it retains its original subtleties and depth. Reading it for the first time, we found ourselves led through a long and dark tunnel, and praying very hard for the glimpse of light that would mark its end.

We are grateful that wounds heal. We are even more grateful for the things on Earth that help wounds heal—family, friends, medicine, money, time. May all who are wounded find the cocoon that provides you with that precious shelter.

Suddenly, Without A Map

by Winnie M. Li

"Can you help me? I think I'm lost and don't know where I'm going."

"A fifteen-year-old boy says this to me, and there is something odd and untraceable in his pale eyes as he approaches. I'm walking through Colin Glen Forest Park in West Belfast on a Saturday afternoon. As a Chinese-American, I'm an obvious foreigner in this part of town, so it's strange that he would ask me for directions. But I do my best to help anyway.

"Over in that direction is the Falls Road..." I start to explain.

It's a beautiful spring afternoon in 2008, and I'm in a good mood, having just begun to unwind from three busy days of meetings and conferences in Northern Ireland. Tomorrow, I'll be flying back to London to attend the red carpet premiere of a film I'd helped to produce. Today, I've set aside time to hike along an eleven-mile trail described in my Lonely Planet guidebook, starting in this city park and extending up to the north of Belfast. It's a little reward for myself, a chance to bask in nature, and escape the whirl of social events and work commitments which make my life so busy.

I am twenty-nine years old, driven, professional, ambitious, and I have a Plan.

That Plan does not include getting randomly assaulted and raped by a fifteen-year-old stranger.

In fact, the Plan was all together different, a script for achievement and happiness. It had been instilled in me by my immigrant parents, who moved to America as graduate students from Taiwan. And it went something like this: study hard, get into a good university (Harvard, preferably), establish a prosperous career, start a family, make your parents proud.

Most of my life, I'd developed variations on the Plan. Like when I decided to study Folklore and Mythology at Harvard, instead of preparing for medical school. Or when I became addicted to travelling on my own, backpacking through Germany at the age of nineteen so I could write for a travel guidebook. Or when I moved to London at twenty-three, without a work visa, chasing down the slim possibility of working for a film producer I had met once. Most of the time I managed to get things to work, somehow balancing my over-achiever ethic with my thrill for adventure and the unknown.

But that afternoon, this fifteen-year-old boy in Belfast presented a completely different kind of unknown to me.

After all, no one ever plans to put "Rape Victim" on their CV.

None of this is on my mind as I continue hiking in the park that afternoon, the fifteen-year-old still trying to make incoherent conversation with me. In my typical driven fashion, I am eager to get on with the trail, and I don't want this kid tagging along. But every few minutes, he keeps showing up, as if he's playing some kind of game, following me deeper and deeper into the less populated parts of the park.

An uncomfortable feeling tells me there's something weird going on, but I'm not going to stop hiking just because of some annoying kid.

And when I confront him for the third and final time, by the edge of the forest, it's too late. There's nobody else around, and the nearest busy road is five hundred metres away, across an empty, derelict wasteland. As he emerges from the bushes this time, an unfamiliar panic rises in my gut.

"Do you like to have sex outdoors?" he asks suddenly.

Something unnatural skips in the beat of my heart. "No," I say firmly, and I turn instantly towards the busy road.

But then, it's as if a switch has been flipped.

"Stay right there, bitch!" he screams, and now I see a feral anger burning in his pale eyes. "Don't move!"

Taken aback, I try to make frantic sense of the situation. Could I take him on in a physical showdown? If it weren't for my backpack, I'd be sprinting for the busy road already, but in my confusion, I hesitate.

Then he's grabbing me, pulling me towards the bushes, and I'm pushing to get free. Don't lose your footing, I warn myself. But the ground underneath is tricky—loose stones rattling over upturned earth, and it gives way below me, my hiking shoes slipping on the pebbles.

I am thrown to the mud—and the next moment, he is on top of me, his hands at my throat, his fist rising up to strike me on the head.

Some thirty, forty minutes later, I am covered in mud and bruises. I haven't blacked out, the way they do in movies, to conveniently cut out the unpleasant part. I've been conscious through it all, and some engine-like survival instinct has kicked in, constantly reassessing the situation, trying to figure out the best solution, the most practical way to act. Have years of project management as a film producer, a decade of experience as a solo backpacker, taught me anything? I must improvise. There is no script to this. No carefully devised Plan. Nowhere on the map did the Lonely Planet mark out that here, at this point in the trail, I would encounter a troubled boy with psychopathic tendencies.

So thirty, forty minutes later, he has left—having made no attempt to take my wallet, my iPod, my phone, my watch. He got what he came for, and now he's gone.

Only then do I allow myself to cry, as I sit by the side of the path, that engine still churning away, trying to decide what to do next. Part of me wants to get up and continue the trail, strike out for the hills and escape—just so I can pretend it never happened. Yet somehow I know that realistically, that's not the responsible thing to do. My mind is unable at that moment to piece together the word "rape." But I know I need medical attention, and I know this boy deserves to be caught. So I make my decision.

Feebly, I make my way across the derelict wasteland towards the busy road. I call a friend. She calls the police. When the police find me twenty minutes later, there is the thick drawl of Belfast accents asking me if I'm OK, if I can show them the crime scene, if I can describe my attacker. That engine is racing now, spitting out details, functioning on overdrive to provide the police as much information as possible. But the heart of me—the real me—has gone into hiding. Completely shell-shocked. Silently grateful when my friends arrive, to hold my hand throughout the subsequent eight hours of questions and exams. But otherwise mute, stunned, trapped in a surreal daze.

That daze lasted for months, even years, after the day of the attack. It's as if a giant knife had just been ripped through my insides, gutting me clean, so that I was a mere shell of who I had been. This proxy, shell-like version of me went about living the ruins of my life, handling the mundane, day-to-day tasks of the crime procedural, the endless medical follow-up, maintaining any previous resemblance my life now had to the one before the attack.

The irony of it all, is that I had been invited to Belfast as some kind of honour. Years before, I'd been a George Mitchell Scholar, selected to serve an ambassadorial role as an American studying in Ireland on a prestigious fellowship. That week in 2008, I'd been flown to Belfast to attend a special symposium commemorating the tenth anniversary of the peace process in Northern Ireland. I used the opportunity to schedule a few meetings for an upcoming film project I hoped to produce there that year.

One minute, you're a busy, ambitious film producer with a hyperactive social and work life. The next minute, you're a rape victim, covered in mud and bruises, the topic of tomorrow's lurid headline, another unnamed statistic in the crime log.

The absurdity is not lost on me, a day after the rape, as I struggle to attend the red-carpet premiere of a film I'd worked on. I've walked red carpets before, I'd been to the Oscars when one of our films was nominated. Working in the media, I am all too aware of the importance of image, of presenting yourself well, of projecting success and confidence. But when a truth this harsh is suddenly thrust upon you, can you maintain the right kind of image and remain genuine to yourself?

Less than twenty-four hours after the attack, I'm on a plane back to London. I've told my boss what has happened, but it's the first Leicester Square premiere for one of our films, and after years of hard work, I'm not going to allow some fifteen-year-old jerk prevent me from enjoying this.

Only, of course, he already has.

A friend meets me at the airport, takes me home, helps me into a diaphanous gown which a designer has lent me for the occasion. Long, white, in a classical Grecian style—it's a pity I can't even appreciate it this evening. My multiple bruises are very visible, but I ignore them as I struggle to put my hair up. Another friend meets me in Leicester Square and takes me down the red carpet. Thankfully we're too late for any press or public to care who we are.

In the cinema, I am seated next to a film director I've worked with many times before. He asks me casually how I am, unaware of what's happened. I hesitate. I ask him if he wants to know the truth, and he answers, yeah, sure why not. I tell him.

Shocked, he doesn't know what to say, and eventually blurts out, gauchely: "What, he was just a kid and you couldn't fight him off?"

"No," I say, shaking my head. And that conversation is over.

After the screening, we make our way to the after-party in a trendy West End club. The low-level lighting helps to conceal my bruises, and I make small talk with the actors from our film, while sipping inventive cocktails and nibbling on canapés. On the outside, I probably seem fine. Inside, I'm hardly there.

The next morning, I start making phone calls to my doctor and the local rape crisis centre, asking what medical and psychological care I should be seeking. There's a glut of work emails in my inbox, and unable to cope, I write to one contact: "I am sorry but over the weekend, I was assaulted and raped. Could you please speak to one of my colleagues about this for the time being?"

Was it unprofessional to write that? Would it have been more professional to say I was "in an accident," when that is so far from the truth? I don't care. I now have greater concerns.

My sister arrives a few days later, having been granted time off from her law firm to fly eleven hours and see me. It is comforting to have her with me as we traipse from one hospital appointment to another. I have just enough energy to negotiate my new medical and legal responsibilities as a rape victim. Once home, I collapse uselessly on the couch while my sister takes care of food, errands, tidies my usually messy room.

We both agree the news of my attack should be kept from our parents. We don't talk at length about it, but somehow we both feel, deep down, that this kind of terrible, unexpected news might be too much for our parents to bear. That they're better off not knowing the truth. Better off thinking their youngest daughter, who graduated Summa Cum Laude from Harvard, who has been single and living on the other side of the world for eight years now, is still happily working towards a rewarding career.

I think for a moment about the kind of grief that would drown my parents if we tell them—my mum's sobbing, my dad's unspoken frustration. And I think it would be better off to spare them that. Their emotional anguish, thousands of miles away, would only make matters worse.

This one, I decide, I will have to handle on my own.

The afternoon of the attack, the police ask me how I would describe myself physically, since they will need to release a physical description of both the victim and the suspected assailant, in a plea for witnesses. I describe myself as "a woman in her mid-to-late-twenties. Chinese-American, slim, with long, black hair."

In Belfast, perhaps the notion of Chinese-American proves too slippery.

The following day, newspaper headlines shout: "Chinese tourist brutally raped" or "A Chinese student attacked and raped in Colin Glen Forest Park". Some journalists contact the Chinese Welfare Association in Belfast and ask it to comment on my attack. The press emphasises that my assault happened four years ago to the day that a local teenage girl was raped and murdered in the very same park. A few days later, on a Belfast radio chat show discussing local crime, the mother of the murdered girl calls in to express sympathy for me. "My heart goes out to that wee Chinese girl," she sighs in her Northern Irish drawl.

Listening to this in my London flat, I laugh wryly. Somehow it's the omission of the word "American" which paints a completely different picture of how I would be perceived. When an old college friend hears this, he shakes his head and smirks: "'Wee Chinese girl'... You know, that's completely not you."

He's right. But then again, if you picture what the media expects a rape victim to be, that's completely not me, either.

Instinctively, I decide not to hide the truth from any of my close friends. However, this immediately forces me to choose whom I consider close enough. Each time I'm asked the simple question "What's up?" should I brave yet another uncomfortable conversation—or put up a completely false façade? I insist on the truth, if I am going to consider any friendship genuine. I even send a mass email out to my friends, explaining what happened, to pre-empt having to tell the same story over and over.

My female friends, both in London and abroad, prove to be amazingly supportive, sympathetic, eager to cook me a meal or send me a care package. Several of them share stories of their own rape, or of their sister, aunt, cousin who had been raped. None of these stories I'd ever heard before.

The men react less helpfully. Unsure of what to say,

some take weeks to email back after I tell them what had happened. Others freeze upon hearing the truth.

It is this awkward reaction I try to avoid, but pretending to be normal in any social situation now seems tantamount to lying to myself. How can I be "normal" when I'm plagued daily by claustrophobia, nausea, unpredictable bouts of crying? I used to be able to backpack through foreign countries on my own. Now, even venturing outside my apartment causes panic. I once could befriend complete strangers on a train. But if a fifteen-year-old boy can do this to you, who can you trust? These days, I can't even handle meeting acquaintances. Or if I do, it involves erecting a thin, flimsy façade of "normality", which threatens to collapse at any moment.

Unfortunately, I have to attend three weddings within six months of my attack. I'm to be a bridesmaid at the wedding of an ex-flatmate in July. A few weeks earlier, her hen weekend kicks off on a Friday night at a louche, opulent nightclub in Camden called Gilgamesh. Earlier that afternoon, I'm scheduled to visit the Southwark Police Station, so I can identify my attacker via a video "I.D. parade". This is the long-distance equivalent of a police line-up: instead of fifteen similar-looking teenage boys lining up behind a pane of one-way glass, they've been videotaped for me to look at. The now-familiar nausea builds up in my stomach as I sit down to watch the I.D. parade—sweaty palms, heart palpitations, the urge to vomit at the mere thought of my attacker.

But then, when his face comes up on the screen, it's like a dart hitting the bull's eye. Bam!—That's him. No question about it. "It's number five," I tell the attending police officer with deceptive calm, as I nervously dent and undent my half-empty Diet Coke can.

Meanwhile, my gut turns inside me.

A few minutes later, while I'm decompressing with a friend in Starbucks, I get a text from another friend on sabbatical. She's on a volunteer mission with her boyfriend in Africa, and she's just gotten engaged.

I text her my congratulations, and then excuse myself from the coffee shop. After all, I have a hen party to attend in a couple of hours. On the bus ride home, I'm shaking— either from the I.D. parade or the dread of attending this hen party, or both. Once home, I descend into tears, sobbing uselessly while fully aware that I'm supposed to be getting ready.

I have to get into a black dress. I have to wear heels. I have to put on make-up.

Is this for real? It feels like parallel worlds, moving from the I.D. parade of my rapist to a hen party. Or from giving my deposition to the police, the morning after my attack, to a red-carpet film premiere in Leicester Square. Are we really meant to be this versatile?

I show up almost two hours late to the hen party.

"Don't worry," Silvia winks at me, aware of my earlier visit to the Southwark Police Station. "You look great, anyway."

And the rest of that evening, I find myself drinking champagne and making mindless small talk, while underneath it all, my engine is working desperately, exhausted, struggling to keep up that façade.

Silvia's wedding is in Slovakia that July, followed by another friend's in Dublin, and then another in Scotland that October. I am happy for all of them, of course, but having to dress up and maintain a certain cheery image becomes a superhuman chore for me. And then, of course, there is the envy. The sharp pain of watching my friends, surrounded by parents celebrating their marriage, pledging their mutual love to someone who is willing to be with them for the rest of their lives.

It's a cliché, but in the midst of it all, I feel very alone.

And as much as I try to avoid it, the questions and the self-doubt start to creep in. The lecture my parents might have given me, if they knew the truth. The speculation that maybe—if I was just that little bit more conventional, if I was the kind of docile daughter of Chinese immigrants who went to medical school, who did what was expected, who allowed herself to be courted by some other Ivy League graduate, who wasn't still single at the age of twenty-nine, who didn't insist on backpacking solo through Europe, or go hiking alone in strange parks for fun—maybe none of this would have ever happened.

But then again, if I was that person, I wouldn't have been me.

And however much I regret having gone into that park on that particular afternoon in Belfast, I still don't regret being who I am.

The old me would have found a certain solace in travel, so I follow that impulse, even though I am unsure what I can handle in my post-traumatic state. Whereas normally I would go somewhere remote, perhaps Third World, I decide to visit friends in the United States for all of August. Making my way from California, to Chicago, New York and Boston, I find comfort in my friends—many of whom are settling into different phases of their lives, getting engaged, starting new families.

On the last day of my trip, I find myself in Harvard Yard. There, I wander wistfully among the familiar greenery and slanting sunlight, the same dignified red-brick-and-grey-stone buildings which I haunted as an undergraduate ten years ago. I watch a few tourists: Asian parents proudly photographing their eight-year-olds on the Harvard campus, as if harbingers of their educational future. Everything seems eerily unchanged, even though I could not be farther from the inexperienced teenager I was when I came here.

After all, it was here where I learned that if you have talent, take charge and strive for what you believe in, you can achieve anything. But they never told you that one day, when you least expect it, a random stranger can destroy your entire sense of self. Life is not always the meritocracy we want it to be. And that is not a lesson they teach you at Harvard.

But in this new, crueler reality, I am still trying to test my boundaries. I discover a budget airline sale and impulsively book a £22 return flight to Nîmes, in the South of France. This is the kind of thing I would have done before the attack—after all, there's a Roman aqueduct near the town that I've always wanted to see.

I consider it a challenge to the new, frightened me. So at some point in mid-October, I find myself checking into a small, family-owned hotel on my own. The hotel sits a stone's throw from the Roman arena, but in the off-season, it's eerie and completely empty, except for me— and one other guest whom I never see, but hear once in a while. On top of that, the family who owns it is going away on vacation the evening I arrive. It's the perfect set-up for a horror movie, I think, as my post-traumatic panic starts to set in. That night, I push a chest of drawers in front of my door, before I crawl into my narrow bed and eventually fall into an uncomfortable sleep.

But the next morning, I find myself standing in front of the Pont du Gard: this ancient Roman aqueduct, rising like some ageless vision from the mist of the River Gardon. It towers over the otherwise empty valley, nearly two millennia old, and I find a certain constancy in the beauty of its massive, three-tiered presence. For a short while, I can almost forget the panic and unease which have been my constant companions since the attack. Just ancient stone, arching over tranquil waters.

On the hills above the Pont, various paths snake into the autumnal forest, and I start to explore them. My old excitement begins to stir. Part of me wants to go further down the path, discover more, see more—but then, the new fear sets in, snapping me back like a leash. The old me would have happily continued down that path, only too eager to explore beyond the next bend. The new me is cowardly, afraid of the unknown—and I turn back, defeated, to the safety of other tourists.

Once back in London, I realise I'm not really up to scratch. I must have been fooling myself to think I could travel on my own—and of course, work is out of the question. Besides, the production company I've run for the past six years has just been struck by the economic crisis and can no longer afford to pay my salary. My already modest income dwindles to nothing. And my career—until now, the driving force in my adulthood—is set adrift.

I sink into a tedious limbo. My hollowed-out shell collapses inward, and becomes a negative void, dragging me down, like a black hole. After six months on the waiting list of the UK's National Health Service, I am finally assessed and diagnosed with Post-Traumatic Stress Disorder. I am prescribed fifteen sessions of Cognitive Behaviour Therapy at the Centre for Anxiety Disorders and Trauma. They are exhausting, and involve endless sets of questionnaires, asking how many times I've had nightmares each week, how many times I've panicked.

But these dark winter months are dominated by the slow ticking of the clock, the inevitable drag towards the moment I have long been dreading—the moment when I take to the stand to testify against my attacker in court. The Belfast police give me what information they can, but by now, the case is in the hands of the Public Prosecution Service, working its way through the bureaucratic processes of the Northern Irish judicial system. I know my attacker has been held in a juvenile detention centre since a week after my assault, and that he has been pleading not guilty. Beyond that, I am told little else, other than that at some point early next year, I must fly back to Belfast to testify in court.

Eventually, the date is set for 8 March 2009.

And so, my entire life becomes a slow, fearful countdown to that dreaded date. Proxy Me flies to Los Angeles to spend a joyless, unmemorable Christmas and New Year's with my parents, who are still unaware of what happened. Other than that, I am mainly confined to a grey, anxious existence in London, pulled so taut with nerves over the impending court date, that I find it impossible to relax, or enjoy anything.

I finally decide to go on anti-depressants. On the advice of my psychologist, I start going to the gym regularly. I take up Buddhist meditation. I play Brickbreaker on my BlackBerry. A lot. Anything to calm me down even slightly from this unrelenting anxiety. But the tension is magnified in my nightmares, and the thought of seeing him in court makes me sick to my stomach.

And yet, I am aware that my nervousness is some heightened version of the tension I felt as a child, in the minutes leading up to a piano recital. The expectation to perform. To not screw up. Even while describing, in detail, in public, the ordeal of my rape, while sitting across from my attacker.

Even now, we can't escape our high expectations. Our exacting definition of success. Will I perform to the best of my abilities in court? That is the question which plagues me the most as the date draws near.

Am I up to it? It's not about him, and it's not about the rape itself. It's about me.

And then, on the morning of 8 March, in a courthouse near Belfast—everything changes within minutes. Waiting for the jury to be selected, I sit with my friends in a separate room, nearly sick to my stomach. I am suddenly told that he has pleaded guilty at the last minute.

"So.... there won't be a trial?" I ask, disbelieving. "I don't have to testify?"

And just like that, my most dreaded moment suddenly vanishes. The whole purpose of my trip to Belfast, the cause of all my months of anxiety is suddenly negated. It feels anticlimactic—and completely surreal.

My friends are jubilant, and I'm flooded with relief. But part of me—perhaps the competitive side of me—feels partially robbed of a showdown, of the chance to actually confront the boy who brought on my past year of misery, and to see justice be done.

Six weeks later, I do get that chance when I'm back in Belfast for the sentencing hearing. This is the final step in the judicial process, and while I am not required to attend, I feel that I want to see this through to the very end. I had set this process in motion the moment I decided to contact the police that afternoon—and to not forget the attack had happened. And now, more than a year later, I would see that process finally completed.

In the meantime, I've fallen ill for the past six weeks, sleeping fifteen hours a day, while my body starts the long journey of recovering from a year of constant anxiety, PTSD and depression. A friend holds my hand as I sit in court that day, and I'm aware of my attacker's family sitting in the same row, ten seats away.

Then, the judge enters the room. We listen as he sentences my attacker (now sixteen years old) to eight years in prison. There is a very clinical, mathematical explanation of how he calculated eight years, based on judicial precedent and the particulars of the case. The police detective next to me remarks that this is a more severe sentence than he had expected. And then the hearing is over.

My attacker's family gathers around their son, who has been sitting in the dock until now. He's just been sentenced to half the length of his current lifetime. Just once, I see him turn his head and look at me, but I don't lock eyes with him. It's over. I do not need to see more. I only want to look ahead from now on.

That evening, my friend and I decide to drink a bottle of champagne while waiting for our flight back to London. Once aboard, we order another half-bottle from the in-flight menu. By the time we're halfway through the flight, we are both roaring drunk. Several of the other passengers look back at us—but I could not care less. This is the first time I've been able to enjoy champagne in over a year. And by God, do I have a reason to celebrate.

Less than two days later, I'm on another budget flight, this time all by myself to Croatia. I've wanted to visit Croatia for years, and now with the completion of the judicial process, all my previous fears about travelling have miraculously been lifted.

I haven't even booked any accommodation, but when I step off the bus in Split, I find myself bargaining with an old man for a private room in the Old Town. My six days in Croatia flash by in a stream of sun-spangled beach and Mediterranean architecture. I marvel at Diocletian's Palace in Split, sun myself on the deck of a ferry, scramble atop the city walls of Dubrovnik. I'm on my own, but that shadow of fear which haunted me in Nîmes is gone in the clarity of the Mediterranean sun.

Nor do I stop there. Emboldened by my rediscovered ability to travel, I join some American friends for a trip to Vietnam and Cambodia. I add on a weeklong stopover in Borneo, just for myself. I watch "orang utans" in awe, snorkel through tropical waters, bond with other backpackers over late-night card games in the middle of the jungle.

Even weddings become gradually more enjoyable for me. I have five to attend that year, in various countries. But with each subsequent wedding, the once-brittle shell version of me is filling out, turning solid and real once more. For the first time in a very long time, I have something to be proud of—the fact that I fulfilled my responsibility as a rape victim, and I've done it well, putting my attacker behind bars. Things would only get better from here.

But not instantaneously. My recovery is gradual. While travel increasingly makes me feel more like the old me, it's not the same in London. Various forms of therapy—physical, holistic, psychological—continue, and I still constantly feel ill and exhausted.

The thought of work doesn't even cross my mind. I fill out the occasional job application, but why work now, when I can enjoy life? When I haven't been able to enjoy life in ages?

Even before the attack, I'd been so dedicated to the notion of working hard, of achieving success (however

I chose to define it), that life itself—when I wasn't travelling—was constantly determined by expectations, accomplishments, obligations.

Now with my attacker sentenced, I realised my only obligations were to myself—to recover and heal. To become the person I wanted to be again, and maybe, be even stronger than before. I felt that if I could survive the last twelve months, and handle that on my own, then I could survive almost anything.

So would I eventually piece together my professional life and somehow resume a meaningful career?

Yes, I would.

Would I one day have the kind of personal and family life I envisioned?

I hoped so.

But I had the whole rest of my life to figure that out, and I knew I could trust myself to perform to the best of my abilities, when the time came.

So for now, I felt I deserved a little time off.

I spent the last three months of 2009 backpacking on my own through Southeast Asia. After my trip to Vietnam in the spring, I realised how easy it was to travel in that part of the world, even how comforting it was to blend in visually, and not to look so obviously foreign. So I booked a cheap flight from London to Bangkok and back, with three months in between (the maximum stay). I wasn't really sure where I'd go during this time, but I knew I'd be able to improvise as I went along.

The day I landed in Bangkok, *The Belfast Telegraph* printed my anonymous article about my experience as a foreigner, randomly attacked and raped while travelling in Belfast. As I sat on Khao San Road, enjoying a Pad Thai and a Beer Chang, and reading a downloaded scan of the article on my BlackBerry, I wondered if any readers of that article would expect I'd be here, about to start a three-month backpacking trip, all on my own.

I smiled as the thought crossed my mind. I'd done my part. I'd been through the worst of it and back, and lived to tell the tale. And here I was, at the start of a new journey, reading my own article in print. Since childhood, I'd always wanted to be a professional writer, but I'd been deterred when my parents warned me about how that job was unpredictable and not lucrative.

But what wasn't unpredictable? Six months ago, when I was agonising about the trial of my rapist, would I have predicted that in September I'd be here, eager to embark on a solo backpacking trip for three months? And twelve months before that, would I have predicted that one spring afternoon in Belfast, I would be assaulted and raped while walking through a park?

Life moves in capricious circles like that, doubling back upon itself, betraying the ground beneath you. You can have your plans and your expectations, but you never know what waits around the next bend. The best you can do is to live in the moment, and to follow your instincts, if the going gets tough. Sometimes you get lost, and sometimes you don't have a map. But most of the time, you don't need one—you learn to trust yourself.

• • •

Winnie M. Li (http://winniemli.com) is a writer and filmmaker. She has achieved multiple accolades for her films, including an Oscar nomination. A former writer for the *Let's Go* travel guide books, Winnie has travelled extensively on five continents. She is currently aiming to finish her comedic first novel, *Fag Hag and Other Fairy Tales*. A Taiwanese-American raised in New Jersey, she studied Folklore and Mythology at Harvard and later moved to Ireland as a George Mitchell Scholar. Winnie served as Head of Development for Ugly Duckling Films in London for nearly nine years and now works in Programming for the Doha Tribeca Film Festival and Doha Film Institute in Qatar. In April 2011 three years after the attack, she hiked the 95-mile West Highland Way in Scotland, on her own.

EDITORS' NOTE

Random Musings

Self help books often emphasise the importance of conscious living: conscious breathing to improve the state of one's mental and physical health, conscious eating to improve the absorption of the food's nutrients, conscious being to appreciate and enjoy the going-ons in your living environment.

Bava's musings made us a little more conscious of and sensitive to the moment—good for the heart, good for the mind and certainly good for the soul. Enjoy.

Random Musings
by Bava Wadhwa

Venus and Vindaloo

venus and vindaloo

a heady combination

attractive to the new and a few

garam masalas

roman piazzas

funny clothing

croissants in the morning

venus vindaloo

a burning planet

for me and who?

on clear nights

after lips and bites

in my supine state
her light penetrates; ameliorates

venus@vindaloo
eyes are red
the soul is blue

love and spice
cum at a high price
exotic aromas, lingering and tantric
burning taste buds, numbed but frantic

venus and vindaloo
clinging under
an Indian moon

Mourning in Hull
I walk down a hill littered with cigarettes and refuse
The air is furious and cold
Sparrows can be heard from near and far
It's morning on my way to Hull
The people line up single file
The nicest Canadians you ever did see
No pushing, no jostling, "after you", a free newspaper
The bus stop on a Friday morning in Hull

Today I don't get a seat
Bouncing and bumping we traverse the river
The resigned faces of the public
Servants to the clock
During morning in Hull

This place is exactly like the next
Indistinguishable cubicles between,
the front, the sides and the behind
back and around
Yet, a few nice corners lined with plants
Turning their face
To morning in Hull

Sitting here in my fabric walls
My screen a link to the virtual world
I contemplate another day of work
Craning my neck for inspiration
From morning in Hull

And now the people are slowly filtering in
The tapping of the keys gets louder and more frequent
Sounds and movement are beginning to change
Until another morning in Hull

The Possibilities are Endless

thermal underwear

hot hot hot

a climbing harness

to hold you in spot

indiglo alarm clock

beeps at cold dawn

moisture wicking

nexus-backed tegralatex

oooh

i like

u lock

with an oversized case

and dark metal block

swix glide wax

cork polish scrape

an altimeter, barometer, electronic compass

with declination adjustment

monitoring the climax rate

Midas Touch

Sometimes Love
Is the colour of bruises

Purple passion
Black affection
Blue legacy

All these marks
Get set
Now go

• • •

Baljit Wadhwa, or Bava as she is known to her family and friends, was born in India but raised in Canada. She studied Molecular Biology at the University of Calgary and Natural Resource Management at the University of Waterloo. An irresistible desire for adventure took her to five cities in ten years, and in 2006 she moved to Washington D.C. to work on sustainable public and private sector investment. Bava currently evaluates international environmental projects but, given the choice, would spend more of her time indulging in her gear fetish, paddling or taking photos while watching the world go by.

EDITORS' NOTE

To Be or Not to Be

To be or not to be? This is a real question for many women. To be one's authentic self? Or to hide certain qualities so as to be more "desirable"? As we get older and more confident, we also move onto shakier ground. Why? Because of the ticking biological clock and the lingering fear that one may forever remain a childless spinster. Of the wanting to be seen and heard but not to create so much shadow and noise that our partners choose to be with someone "less" instead. Less forward. Less active. Less independent.

Isabel's dilemma is shared by many of us. A modern woman with a career, she questions whether her fun, feisty personality—indeed her best qualities—are the reasons why the dream of a life partner (not to be confused with the desire to "have a man" but, rather, the longing for a co-conspirator in the best of senses) remains elusive.

To Be or Not to Be

by Isabel Hagbrink

So it has come to this: I'd be a better date if I were a man. My friend Faith tells me one day, and I believe her: "You'd make a great husband!" Not sure if I should take this as a compliment. Her comment doesn't bode well for my dating game since straight guys aren't usually looking for "great husband" types.

The thing is it's not really my fault. It's Mum's. She apparently raised me to be a great potential hubby—a proactive, organised, resourceful and well-travelled person who knows how to weather-proof windows, assemble IKEA furniture in a jiffy, is on first-name basis with the folks in the local hardware store, and is financially independent to boot.

I'm not sure when it all started. But growing up with an independent mother who whisked me around the world from the tender age of nine probably had something to do with it. I loved meeting new people and cultures, and became an adventurer, whether I liked it or not. And it's been that way ever since.

In my twenties, this meant taking off to Venezuela to write a thesis and do odd jobs. In my thirties, I worked with aid programmes in the Caribbean. Nowadays, as I have more or less settled in Washington D.C., it means that I'm the eternal local explorer, always on the lookout for romantic getaways and cozy new restaurants. Catching the latest artsy flick and finding nearby farms to pick pumpkins for Halloween. Friends from near and far call for advice on what to do and where to go. Newbies in town ask if they can tag along and I am always happy to take them, if they can keep up!

It doesn't stop there. I have quirky personal guides to all my favourite cities, from Barcelona to Miami, Stockholm to Tokyo. God forbid friends should visit Kenya and miss the best little leather shop in Nairobi for that perfect cow hide clutch. Whatever the need or question, call Isabel. I could give you ideas for a great date night in at least ten countries. And if I don't know the answer, I know someone who does.

Unfortunately, there is a downside to these strengths, especially where dating is involved. It's tough to take

Isabel out in town to show her something new. I have to hold back when a guy asks if I have been to that new Japanese restaurant downtown that everyone is raving about, because of course I have. I hate to show my disappointment when the most romantic suggestion for Valentine's is dinner and a movie; I could have thought of so many more exciting things to do. A male friend recently asked me, a bit in awe of everything I did: "How does a man keep you interested?"

I think men feel a tad emasculated. Some years ago, my then boyfriend told me, as he followed me into the street in Cuzco to find a taxi at 6am—late for the train to Macchu Picchu—that "dating you is like dating a man." So, Faith wasn't the only one to notice. Some Peruvians, it seems, are not used to women hailing their own early morning rides either. But after surviving Hurricane George in a flooded apartment in Santo Domingo and getting on with no electricity for weeks, hailing a cab just doesn't seem like a big deal.

I have a friend in Sweden who remarked last summer that he wants to be with a woman he can take under his wing and show the world. He specifically does not want to be with someone who has seen more places around the world than he has. This surprises me as I've always assumed that emancipated Swedish men, in particular, would prefer a woman who can hold her own and carry it too. Of course, different courses for different horses, but what on Earth does this mean for a gal like me?

Realising that a man is more attracted to the damsel in distress than to Miss Independent has been cause for plenty of self-doubt and frustration over the last few years. In my twenties, for example, I had no problem rejecting macho men who appeared to feel threatened by me. I readily dismissed them and their insecurities, happy to wait for someone more mature to come along, confident that my "ideal man" was just around the proverbial corner.

These days however, I increasingly wonder if I might have been following the wrong recipe for love. That perhaps being myself—strong and savvy—and remaining true to my character, is not the best strategy for snagging a man.

I never agreed with the love advice touted in books such as *The Rules*, but I have started to wonder if showing the full strength of my personality early in the relationship is akin to shooting myself in the foot, relationship-wise that is. Should I tone down my personality, at least in the initial phase of a romance? Should I do what I can to boost his ego, let him believe he is right, rather than point out a mistake? For example, if a man takes the wrong turn when driving, do you keep mum or pipe up? I would instinctively let him know, but a lot of my girlfriends would not. Let him be, they'd say. He is the one driving the car.

Meryl Streep wrote in her contribution to Katie Couric's book *The Best Advice I Ever Got* that it took her years to find her true voice. When she did, it wasn't the demure, pretty, softly giggling woman whom she tried on for size as a teenager and whom all the men fell for. That was just an act. Her true temperament, she says, developed later in life—when she became the slightly bossy, opinionated, loud and high-spirited woman she is today. And it scared men off—although it clearly hasn't hampered her career.

I identify with most of those traits she discovered in herself. It's ironic that qualities that make women successful at work are the same things that keep us in long-term singlehood. In order to keep a relationship going, is it possible that strong women must turn off these qualities? Do we need to start tap dancing around men, censoring what we say to make sure that egos are not bruised and using positive reinforcement to make them feel that they are in charge?

What is interesting is that strong men are almost always initially attracted to strong, confident women. At least that is what they tell us. One of the first things that suitors gush about is just how much they're taken by my joie-de-vivre. However, after a few months, things inevitably change.

While we remain active, full of ideas, opinionated and willing to stand up for what we think is right, they start to back off.

I remember an ex-boyfriend telling me, "I compete all day at work; I don't want to compete at home." What brought on the comment I can no longer recall—probably some silly discussion on where to hang a painting in our home—but it hit a nerve.

The solution for many women who share my dilemma has been to hold back and pretend to be less than they truly are one hundred per cent of the time. To let a man make the calls, take the decisions, be the one who drives the relationship, is to preserve that unseen Maginot Line of male territory over which we ladies must not stray. I had a friend who asked me: "Would you rather be right or happy?" implying that many a fight is not worth having. If you are always trying to prove a point, you're engaged in being right instead of being engaged in the relationship, they say. There is a lot of truth in this. A relationship is all about compromise. But "don't sweat the small stuff" is a difficult lesson to learn, especially for Type A personalities.

Most of my female friends battle with this case of split personality daily. They take charge and are successful women at work, but switch off and become less proactive in their more personal relationships. These women run companies but pretend that they can't make dinner reservations.

"Let him be the one to make the plans, don't show him you're too interested, don't take his every call. Play hard to get because men like to chase and they don't want a girl who comes to them too easily," is the kind of well-meaning advice I've heard time and again. But is this really a viable solution? How long must I sustain it? Would this become a life-long pretence or would I go back to my old self when, and if, I marry?

In my years living in Latin America, I saw this scenario being played out over and over: sweet, passive girl marries strong, aggressive man who has chased her for years. After the ring is on the fourth finger, she suddenly shows her true colours and rules the family with an iron fist. But deep in my Swedish soul, I feel that not showing my genuine personality would be the worst kind of dishonesty. I couldn't don a cloak of passivity and play a game of hard-to-get solely for the sake of "catching" a man. For the longest time, I have held on to the belief that the one who is out there for me will want me just the way I am, without subterfuges and deceptions. Feisty, yes! Stubborn, sure! But I'm really a romantic at heart.

It seems the interaction between men and women,

however, is an ancient dance that has remained unchanged in the twenty-first century. A man's instinct is to pursue and conquer a woman. No matter how rational or in tune with modern times we say we are. No matter how much men assure us that they like women being direct and forthcoming. This is simply not the case. Any female who does not abide by the rules of this game makes it that much harder for herself in trying to get the man.

That last realisation comes from a hard-learned lesson. Once I was in a serious relationship with a difficult, traditional man and, consequently, adjusted my personality to fit his. To avoid upsetting him, I stopped chatting with people in the grocery store and repressed my curious, bubbly personality. Eventually, it got to be more than I could handle and I broke it off. Some time later, when he attempted to rekindle our relationship, I refused, knowing that I did not like the timid wall flower I had become while with him.

But where does that leave women like me? Our mothers were pioneers in breaking the mold *and* the glass ceiling, yet we are the first generation of women expecting, and who are expected, to have it all. We have shown that we are the equals of men—we can get a great education and a respectable job—so why is it so hard to achieve the happy home life too? We've been told to reach for the sky but developing the personality needed for a successful career seems actually to become an obstacle to a long-lasting relationship. Many of my more open-minded male friends will tell me I am exaggerating, but I am sorry to say that I speak from experience.

Ultimately my experiences have answered the important question: can I play the game? The answer is no, I can't play it well or, at least, maintain it for long. I have discovered that as frustrated as I am about being single, I would rather embrace the lonely state than be stuck in a role that smothers and makes me resent both my partner and myself. Centuries ago, Shakespeare, who knew a thing or two about human nature, said: "This above all: to thine own self be true. It must follow that you cannot then be false to any man."

His words were not written to reflect modern relationships, but are apt. It boils down to this: maybe it's a good idea to tone it down a notch or two in your relationship with a man, especially if you're typically quite critical. We can all strive to be kinder and gentler, to be more patient and accepting of people. But we mustn't play games or assume roles that are not in line with who we are, that we do not feel natural and comfortable with, because sooner or later that lack of comfort will be the ruin of anything good we might lay claim to in a relationship.

So, what does the future hold for me in love and life? Only time will tell. After every failed relationship I feel like throwing in the towel and protecting my shredded, aching heart. Giving up on men entirely. Having kids on my own, as some of my beautiful, independent and strong women friends have done. But then I meet a wonderful guy, things brighten up and I decide to give it another go, all the while remaining true to who I am and what I want... and that I'd rather wait than be anyone other than myself.

• • •

Isabel Hagbrink was born in Sweden. Her mother being a diplomat, she globetrotted a fair bit, living in Poland and Pakistan before going to boarding school in Sweden. Isabel studied finance and economics at the Stockholm School of Economics, and received a Masters Degree in International Relations from Johns Hopkins University/SAIS in Washington D.C. She has worked at the Inter-American Development Bank in project finance and in external communications, as well as in the private sector with projects that reduce greenhouse gas emissions. Isabel lives in Washington D.C., where she is presently the Senior Communications Officer of the World Bank's Carbon Finance Unit. On any given evening, you'll find her biking around the city, enjoying the warm breeze in search of adventure, small or big.

EDITORS' NOTE

Leadership Reflections

So much has been written about leadership that one can conclude there is no fixed formula to becoming a leader. While it is challenging to define, it is not difficult to recognise good leadership when we have it and to feel it instantly when there is a leadership void.

Swaady is a petite lady who possesses an iron will and boundless energy, unfettered by the "bling" of her career successes to date. Through her reflections, we get a glimpse of how she is translating experiences into an ambition to shape the Continent where she is from. Rather than escaping her past, she has chosen to confront the challenges that wrought her childhood. This is a mark of courage and the symbol of a leader.

Leadership Reflections

by Swaady Martin-Leke

"Come to the edge," he said. They said, "We are afraid."
"Come to the edge," he said. They came. He pushed them...
and they flew."
– *Guillaume Apollinaire*

Twelfth April 1980: President W. Tolbert of Liberia was brutally murdered in a military coup by Master Sergeant Samuel Doe, a twenty-eight-year-old illiterate. A few days later, Tolbert's cabinet members were publicly executed. They were tied to poles on a beach in the capital, Monrovia, and shot. Subsequently, Doe suspended the constitution and took over power. This coup started a vicious circle of violence, instability and impoverishment: a descent into hell familiar to many Africans.

I was about three years old then, and my family had settled in Liberia six years before. The fears, the tears: the night's silence was often interrupted by random shots and screams. We hid under the beds, terrorised, clinging to each other and breathing shallowly to make no noise. In our imagination, vandals were bursting into the house, ripping us out of our hiding places to torture and kill whoever they found. Day after day, night after night, we played the same movie in our heads.

Yet, in the midst of this uncertainty my life was punctuated by a well-organised schedule of meals, silent plays and naps. The smile and love of my mother was my sky and my world.

As soon as the airport reopened, my family fled Monrovia, leaving everything behind—including my father—to find refuge in Senegal, where my mother had some family. For a year we lived at my uncle's before emigrating to Côte d'Ivoire to start a new life.

What do you remember when you are only three years old and pushed to the very edge of life?

Memories are blurry, scattered in the labyrinths of unconsciousness. My child brain has locked the fears and horrors of civil war somewhere very deep, from where they cannot resurface. There are images but the sequences cannot be traced back. What remains vivid are the consequences and the impact such events have had on my life.

18 December 2009: Almost thirty years after the Liberian coup and slightly older than Doe when he overthrew Tolbert, I now live in South Africa. I am one of only a few regional female leaders at General Electric, one of the world's largest companies, and I have just signed a landmark contract between the company and the South African national railway to supply one hundred locomotives. This is one of the largest contracts GE has signed to date on the African continent. By doing this, we will help South Africa and Africa as a whole make a technological leap in infrastructure building and also strengthen local skills.

Our African collective history is filled with countless lost futures, wasted childhoods and brutal passages into adulthood. Ten years ago, I had accepted my first job at GE as an internal auditor for the Consumer Finance division. To go from the ashes of civil war in Liberia to a regional leadership role in GE, I had to decide whether to look at life as a glass half empty or half full. Whether to let the traumas of such human tragedy haunt and drag me down, or to choose to overcome them.

I am a self-motivated optimist. I work hard, and give the best I can. I don't expect anything from anyone, whether in life or my career. If I am not satisfied with a situation, I will either deal with it, fix it, or walk away for better shores.

I remember that I was once a refugee. I felt unrooted, relentlessly looking for "home", a precious treasure that cannot be taken for granted. After travelling the world, living in more than ten different countries in thirty years, I realise that you can never find home in a place. It is within you, and I have carried it with me all along.

"Home" is your soul.

This knowledge grounds me and helps me put things in perspective. Too many times, we give undue importance to things which don't really matter in the bigger scheme of things. Would that injustice experienced in the workplace really matter if we were about to die? And, so, going back to the essentials of life, remembering what matters is vital if you want to maintain your sanity in the ruthless corporate world.

Destiny is a dice. You throw as best as you can, and then take responsibility for the outcome. You will never fully understand why your fortune has been different from that of your neighbour. You were the same age and had the same promising future, but her family only escaped fifteen years into the conflict. With no resources, she was never able to complete her education and she went on to be a refugee in Côte d'Ivoire. She scraped a living juggling several jobs. She died last month for lack of healthcare, three hundred kilometres away from Abidjan.

I escaped and went on to a life full of unexpected opportunities and great successes. I am humbled and grateful. Every success is a blessing. And every failure is an opportunity to learn. Learn and move on quickly!

I learned that material things don't matter, as everything you have can disappear overnight. The villa we once lived in faded into one room shared with my mum and brother. The toys I once accumulated were burned to ashes in a second. Material things are ephemeral: they don't determine your value as a human being. I will never search for riches nor let them define me, but I seek constantly to enrich my soul. Whether struggling to make ends meet or earning a big executive salary, my inner peace and happiness are not shaken.

I am free.

I discovered that hope and faith can never be lost. Left behind, my father would live through a series of civil wars in Liberia, Guinea, Nigeria and Sudan. I corresponded with him for a few years, then lost sight of him for two decades. For twenty years, I prayed that I would not die before I saw him again: and then one day, miraculously, I found him. The love and connection between us had remained intact.

I have become a knower, not anymore a believer. I would never lose sleep over planning my life or career. I have an end goal and a direction, but I find it helpful to remain constantly open to change and embrace it when it knocks at my door.

Nothing is constant but change. And change can be a beautiful thing.

Like so many other such leaders, Doe failed us Africans: he failed his people, his country and his continent. He failed to step up to his responsibility, the responsibility of making a positive contribution to our history and people. How could a young African leader throw his country and people into such chaos, chaos that would end only twenty-five years later when Africa elected its first ever female head of state: Ellen Johnson-Sirleaf?

Yet the same country that produced Doe also produced Sirleaf—the two leaders could not be any more different. Through Sirleaf's leadership, national hope has been revived, Liberia's reputation and credibility have been restored, and tremendous progress has been made in achieving development goals.

Sirleaf is passionately committed to the cause, deeply grounded in strong moral and humanist values. There is no doubt that her empowering and participative leadership, as well as her genuine interest in her people, has helped turn Liberia around and raise the nation.

How many other Sirleafs can Africa produce—women who would change the destiny of a nation and a continent? Women who are great thinkers, great innovators, great entrepreneurs, great achievers and great leaders?

I recognise that the importance of leadership cannot be underestimated, as one's future depends greatly on one's leaders. One person can change the course of your life and who you become. I seek to become a true leader—someone who motivates, inspires, empowers and, above all, serves others with unyielding integrity. I am purposeful. What matters is the cause, not me. I will not indulge in self-pity.

My parents never encouraged bitterness, resentment nor helplessness for any of the dramas of Africa and its bad leaders. On the contrary, they challenged me to be part of the solution. The continent will not change if we, as Africans, are not making this change happen. We have no alternative but to work towards positive transformation with determination.

Through my upbringing, they helped me build an unwavering confidence in myself and a deep sense of purpose grounded in spirituality. They were advocates of the "African Renaissance" and Pan-Africanism. My brother and I were raised on stories of great African leaders such as Soundjata Keita and Kwame N'Krumah. They made sure we had a strong sense of "African-ness" and "African pride". They nurtured a resilient consciousness of the role we must play within the bigger scheme of things, and especially in Africa.

"When you are born African, you are born with a responsibility," my dad would say. This message stuck with me throughout the years, and my life choices have subsequently always been very intuitive. There was never a doubt in my mind that I would come back to Africa to be an agent of positive change. I set up my life objectives at a very young age, and these have never changed.

It was always about transforming my continent.

When I started my career at GE, the Global CEO of the division invited me to his office for a fifteen-minute mentoring session. He left me with a piece of advice which has shaped my career: "Always do something you are passionate about. This is the only way to excel in whatever you are doing."

Finding your passion is like falling madly in love. I am passionately in love with Africa, and this helps me go through the challenges of corporate life. I have been ready to accept all the hardships that come with it, but I never compromise on the end-goal: making a positive impact in Africa. Whether it is in what I do—working on sustainable infrastructure building, skills development, technology transfer, women's empowerment, environmental conservation, education at large—or by developing myself as a positive role model for those around me, the focus remains the same: a better Africa for all.

Today there are less than ten women heads of state out of one hundred and ninety-five countries. In the private sector, only one percent of the CEOs of the world's top five hundred companies are women. In Africa, this number is probably reduced by more than half. It is also very obvious at regional and international gatherings that women are always in the minority. Organisers of events struggle to bring diversity to the panels and participants. Whether in the public or private sector, the low representation of women in leadership positions remains an issue.

As women, we must make use of whatever experience we face throughout our life, positive or negative, to propel ourselves to higher grounds where we will make a lasting and impactful difference. How are these experiences shaping us as leaders? How will we get rid of the fear of failure—the sense that we cannot make it to the top? Sometimes being pushed off the edge creates the opportunity for us to fly.

• • •

Swaady Martin-Leke, an Ivorian-French-American, is an "Afropolitan" global leader, entrepreneur and author. After an illustrious career at General Electric fulfilling leadership roles in Europe, USA, Middle East and Africa, she realised her dream to capture true African luxury and created YSWARA, Curator of Precious African Teas, a brand that is truly African in origin, nature and tradition. Beyond being a repository of African heritage craftsmanship, YSWARA participates in the development and empowerment of farmers and artists—especially women—by providing them routes to market for their products and keeping the value-add in Africa. In 2011, Swaady was named "New Leader of the Future" by the Forum of Crans Montana and was awarded the prestigious Archbishop Desmond Tutu Leadership fellowship in 2012.

EDITORS' NOTE

Living Love, Loving Life

Sometimes we want so much to believe that things can be perfect, and that love will conquer all so long as we give it a chance. We wait patiently for our turn, and dance with joy when it comes! We trust our emotions, our judgment, and take a leap of faith. After all, what is life without hope? And what is hope without dreams? The storm of butterflies in our stomachs is incessant, its loud humming crowding out the voice in the head screaming that things are wrong!

For any woman who has lived life by her own rules, strong enough never to surrender without a fight, the biggest risk can be ignoring the signs and trying too hard. Stubbornly fixing things that have started to unravel irreparably. Sometimes being strong means not persisting in one "happily ever after tale" and moving on to write a new and perhaps better story.

Living Love, Loving Life
by Caroline Barrow

So you're having a long distance relationship. Long distance meaning that you live in one country, England, and your boyfriend of three years lives in another, the US. It's an eight hour journey between London and Washington D.C. Even if the jet stream is kind and the flight occasionally doesn't take more than five hours, the distance is unbearable. You miss each other, anxious for the next chance to hold, to touch, to feel. But you make do with what technology has to offer, talking several times a day by phone, chatting on Skype, "sexting".

He is overwhelmed with the attention and love you have shown him. He can't keep his mind off you. And you can't stop thinking about him either. You count the days and nights to when you'll see each other next. He drives around with a picture of you in his truck for all to see.

Then, one day, he gushes that you are everything he has ever wanted in a woman, a partner, a future wife! This is it for him! At thirty years old, he's had more than his fair share of fun and is ready to settle down. With you.

A single mother in her mid-thirties (yes, five years older), you broke up with your daughter's father before she was born. So you know what it means to work hard and pay your way, balance the demands of a career with childcare, manage expenses. Above all, you're no-nonsense—like the countless generations of West Indian women who have come before you. Your sisters, cousins, aunts have passed on their tales—those-men-dis, those-men-dat, dem-no-good. So, you're not the kind of woman to idolise, to daydream about unbreakable love, to put a man before anything, to fall for a sweet-talker with no substance! But, when you met him some two years before, all the preconceptions changed. You tripped, fell and darn well went spiralling into lala-land. Like a dizzy teenager. Without a doubt. He is the love of your life, and you, his. You're on the verge of an exciting new journey, and it feels like a fairy tale.

Back in London, you've been ignoring interest from other men. And that's no easy feat. Without sounding big-headed, you know that you're gorgeous and there is no shortage of attention from the opposite sex. "Hey baby, can I talk to you?" "Damn, girl, you've got beautiful eyes!" "Umm, could we have a drink one evening after work?" Opportunity abounds to flirt with everyone, from the new person in your office to the bobby on the street. Hard as they try, you resist the flattery, the advances, subtle or otherwise. After all, you are preparing yourself for the day when you will be with this man. To move from London— the place you know and the home you love—and join him on the other side of the Atlantic. To leave your friends and family. To uproot your young daughter. It's worth it, however. Once you're together, the constellations will be aligned and everything will be perfect!

It takes a year for you to get organised. You change jobs within the company, switching to a more international role to smooth your career transition. Days are filled with getting the house you own rented out, packing your things, giving bits and bobs away to family and friends, selling valuables on eBay. Moving is no easy task, particularly while trying to orchestrate a wedding in Hawaii at the same time.

Planning a wedding is hectic in the best of circumstances. It's even worse when the ceremony is miles away, with you as the only person in the driving seat. Henry asked to let him know where and when to go. He's not interested in the finer details, neither the girlie stuff nor the costs involved. He's been laissez-faire about expenses and mumbled that he'd not contribute. Perhaps, blinded by the excitement of flowers, bridal gowns, hair styles and other wedding frills, you fail to question his motivations (or lack thereof). His only responsibility is to buy the rings (his included). Given that he didn't give you an engagement ring, it is the least he could do.

The big day is fast approaching. Three days beforehand, you have a minor setback regarding the immigration papers from the US Embassy. Could this be a sign? Is God trying to convey a message? Maybe. But, not one to give up that easily, especially not where bureaucracy is concerned, you push on. Finally they grant you a fiancée visa for travel to the USA with the intent of getting married within three months. Success!

Some family and friends make it to Hawaii to celebrate with you. A couple of weeks later, you arrive in Washington D.C. and, despite the excitement, something feels amiss.

Maybe it's the incessant noise from the buses zipping up and down the busy street outside that feels a million decibels louder than your quaint cul-de-sac in the outskirts of London. Of course, this isn't the biggest of cities, but it is a city nonetheless, and a real change. Or perhaps it's the dull surroundings of your husband's so-called family home?

Wait, could it be the house?

Probably over a century old, your new home is badly in need of repairs—from the floor to the roof, the outside porch to the kitchen, and not forgetting the bathroom. The attic is a health hazard; one could literally break a leg trying to manipulate the tiny, jagged stairs. Raccoons that have apparently set up camp in between the roof and the attic walls scuttle around at night, chasing each other to find distraction from their macabre situation. It'll only be a matter of time before one of them comes crashing through the ceiling!

Downstairs is no better. Every window is cracked, and the poor air conditioner struggles to keep even a small room cool in the unbearable summer heat. Shoes are a must lest you get splinters from the squeaking floorboards. You can literally dim the lights just by plugging in the iron. Not even the rodent stayed; after spotting one casually scuttling across the dining room, you're pretty sure that it left for good.

The house was owned by Henry's mother, but he had lived there for at least ten years. I soon discovered that my mother-in-law was no easy landlord. We were to fork out two thousand dollars a month to live there. After an initial sense of shock, I accepted it and even started to fix the place up. Pulling myself together, I got busy with making the surroundings more liveable for my new family—buying curtains, rugs, linens, pictures and new house wares. Henry didn't seem to care. He was happy with the way things were and made no effort to pitch in.

Things went from bad to worse, and not just in the home décor department. Henry's true colours slowly emerged.

For starters, I found out that the gas and electricity were on a "hook up". Having always paid my bills, this concept was new to me; in fact, it took me a while to fully comprehend that this meant that the utilities were supplied through an illegal connection facilitated by a friend of Henry's. Can you believe that, in the capital of the world's only superpower, someone was actually connecting his house to a power distribution cable? It is a miracle that we weren't electrocuted in the process. The upside was that, we didn't have a single cold day in winter; the house was always perfectly toasty—all at zero cost. As could be expected, however, the smart set-up only lasted so long. Nine months on, the utilities found out, came knocking at the door and promptly issued a one-thousand-five-hundred-dollar fine.

Then there was the issue of what he did for a living. Henry runs a small construction firm together with a very wealthy business partner. I was always told that things were going well with government contracts and word-of-mouth-referrals for everything from odd jobs to renovations (how ironic, given our own living situation!) and sprucing up a derelict property to turn around a quick profit. What I didn't know was how he really made his money or made up for a short fall when business was bad. Without ever understanding the details, it was enough to know that things weren't kosher.

And it was only a question of time before I discovered his other weaknesses. Henry's former roommate had a key to the basement, and would arrive there unannounced, often before Henry got home, to start an evening of "smoking". They sat there for hours, giggling like a couple of teenagers while the stench of weed crept up the stairs, much to my dismay.

I sometimes laugh out loud at how much the place was like Fawlty Towers. But the truth of the matter is that it was deeply depressing. Unaware of what was to come, my five-year-old daughter and I had moved to this, all in the name of love?

Alas, there we have it. What you now know is that newly married Henry, young entrepreneur, Mr. Perfect, is a weed-smoking, plain idle man-child, who somehow managed to throw this streetwise Cinderella for a loop. Entrenched in his "bachelor life", holed-up in a barely liveable bachelor pad, he has no clue what it means to live life by the book, to be married, to be a stepfather and to have any measure of maturity in his life. He expresses no intent to learn either.

It's now your first Thanksgiving, the Great American family holiday where giving thanks for all you have means much. Instead of doing so, you dwell on your misfortunes and ask yourself, "What the hell happened, Caroline? How could this have gone so wrong?" Over dinner with his family, your ears burn with all the talk of this relatively new migrant family gushing that America is the best place on Earth—most likely because they haven't been anywhere else. You smile and stay sociable; they won't and shouldn't see your confusion, your pain, your anger.

After a few hours of pretence, you take the occasion to become resolute, to double-down with determination to make things right once again. You take a deep breath and commit to making your marriage worth the time, energy, expense and enthusiasm that you gave your courtship. You hold out until Christmas—a month later. You're excited about receiving a gift that says for the first time ever "To my wife..." That anticipation is short lived, however. No card. The present is a sales receipt for fragrance bought online on Christmas Eve.

The new year arrives. New Year, New Hopes, New

Dreams. Perhaps your positive attitude is paying off? Things have suddenly improved, and Henry steps up his game by working extra hard. He tells you that he has planned on retiring at age thirty-five and has an abundance of government contracts awaiting his business. Things will take off and he plans on moving soon, on buying a house with the cash; only poor people need mortgages, he says. You hold a nine to six job at a large international media company with worldwide reach, but he's determined to be the man of the house. So, he heads off to work early each morning with a confident smile on his face.

It is not long before things start to feel wrong again. Suddenly, you're not sure how long he spends in the house during the day while you're at work, but he's always there before you get back. At some point in time, Henry starts leaving home again late afternoon and is now gone until past midnight coming back in at two, three, four, sometimes five in the morning—creeping in through the basement door and sometimes sleeping there for fear of waking you up. What is going on? Is he working night shifts? Could it be that his contracts require him to work when office buildings are closed? There is a pattern to his comings and goings, and it has nothing to do with the working hours of federal employees.

You look more closely into his personal affairs—telephone calls, paper documents. You listen more closely to what he says as he often forgets things, his stories changing with the wind. Where and whenever he can cover himself, he does. Where he can't, his mother makes up a story for him.

Then it comes out. He has been sleeping with someone more his type; street-raised, immature, desperate for attention. She knows that he is married but that's part of the attraction. What is the attraction for him? Who knows? You try to analyse it, to convince yourself that this must be a mistake. I mean, he's messing around with her? At some point, your head clears. The "fix it" approach hits a wall. You understand that there is nothing to mend. You've been blind and things have been broken to a point well beyond repair, beyond what is acceptable. You make up your mind that this marriage is over. You just have to figure out how to and when to leave it while ensuring you have everything you need to walk away.

The plans are now in motion to get out of hell and regain your sanity. To refocus and get back to who you were before he crept into your life. Thankfully, this is your specialty. You save some money, secure a job, muster the support of family and friends and find an apartment. You sit tight and wait until your paperwork is intact so that it is safe enough for you to leave. You want no risk that he could destabilise the life that you are building for your daughter. He could cry wolf and jeopardise your immigration process. You execute your plan to leave and are gone from the house within a week. After the required six-month waiting period, you file for divorce.

The nights filled with fear, with confusion, and with tears slowly become brighter. Your strength returns. The power that you realise you had given away through an innocent desire to live a dream comes back. You press reset—focusing on yourself, your family, on maintaining your independence through a career. You're on stable ground again.

Many of us think that perfection exists. I did. He did. Didn't they make us read Snow White and Sleeping Beauty in pre-school? Weren't our bedtime stories all about difficulties overcome and happily ever afters? So unfair when you think about it, as reality can be an altogether different matter. Especially when it all starts with a long distance relationship where there is ample room to be taken for a ride in a shining carriage.

As I think about telling this story to my daughter when she is old enough to hear it, the message will not be that there can be no happiness. Rather, Damsel can meet Prince Charming but they may not dance together into the sunset. Sometimes, one of them sees the light and decides that she is worth more than he can give and is better off not necessarily on her own but definitely without him.

• • •

Caroline Barrow was born in England to Guyanese parents. She studied Business Management at Thames Valley University in London and has worked in account management for over fifteen years. She juggles a busy schedule, somehow managing to exceed sales targets, get her children where they have to be, and find time for a girls' night out every few weeks. Caroline is very passionate about travel and exposes her children to different cultures from around the world. Her dream is to one day help middle school aged children within her community experience different cultures through her Wheel Barrow Foundation which was launched in June 2012. While Caroline now lives and raises her two young children in the United States, she still calls London home.

EDITORS' NOTE

Distant Rainbow

A famous Japanese saying goes:"The journey from Kamakura to Kyoto takes twelve days; if you travel for eleven days but stop on the twelfth, how can you admire the moon over the capital?"

As Deepa's story shows, life is a journey full of twists and turns, ups and downs. The experience of this winding path is what we choose to make of it. Even in the worst of circumstances, and at the lowest point of our despair, there is always a glimmer of hope and way forward that can and often does lead us to a much better place. It takes faith, spirituality and confidence in one's ability—in this case, Deepa's education. If only the human spirit persists, if only the heart believes, if only we dare walk courageously onward, there will be a rainbow on the horizon. It just takes time to emerge.

Distant Rainbow

by Deepa Hazrati

The year was 2009, the month February. I was swept by waves of exhilaration and anxiousness as I walked towards the airport. My pace was quick and my stomach fluttered with butterflies. I was about to embark on a new life.

I was on my way to Canada from India. It was the first time I was travelling alone out of the country. I had been married seven months earlier in a traditional Hindu ceremony. "The boy" was in Canada and his family was Indian. As per tradition, I stayed in India with his mother after the wedding until my immigration papers arrived. Thankfully, I got the visa without much ado and, seven months later, was on my way to Canada to join my husband.

Like any young new bride, I dreamed of my knight in shining armour—this loving, courageous man in a country where so many of my brethren have headed to live a better life. We could now build the home of our dreams, create a world of love, surrounded by friends and a family of our own.

As you can probably already guess, reality, however, was not quite a bed of roses.

As a child, I was shy. Brought up in a typical Indian middle class family, my parents were simple honest folk. They raised my two siblings and I to be sincere and hardworking people. However, our humble home environment did not stop me from dreaming big. Life should be expansive and beautiful, I thought. And, with my parents' constant encouragement, I reached for the moon.

My childhood days were filled with the ordinary activities of a young girl: studying hard, chatting with friends, laughing and nurturing my hopes for the future. Though a weak constitution made it challenging for me to perform well in school, I was undeterred.

When I was twelve years old, my elder sister introduced me to the philosophy of Nichiren Daishonin, a twelfth century Japanese Buddhist reformer. While I was too young to really understand the difficult concepts of Buddhism, what attracted me to this faith was reading about personal transformation through a steady focus on what one wants in life, and never just "letting things happen". I lived with the spirit, engrained within, that there is a larger world out there, and believed in the importance of self-empowerment and helping others. As Mahatma Gandhi says: "Be the change you wish to see in the world." Through the regular regimen of praying and perseverance, I was able to juggle the challenges of life. Little did I realise that these small victories were preparing me for the harsher realities ahead.

One early breakthrough that can be attributed to my faith came when I was trying to make it to the top of my school while struggling with my health. I was an above average student, yet refused to let go of the desire to be the best. I still remember that deep sense of joy at being ranked first in my undergraduate college and fourth in the entire university, after years of hard work. That year, I was presented with nine prizes, including the Girl of the Year for getting the maximum number of awards!

I successfully completed my undergraduate and graduate programmes in Environmental Science and made it through the onerous Ph.D exams required for entry into a prestigious Indian University. I made it to the top three to qualify for a junior research fellowship and University Grants Commission. I was thus able to lecture in the university and pursue my research with a scholarship.

Soon after starting my coursework, I got engaged. I

flew to Canada, leaving behind my family, friends and studies—all with the hope of realising a new chapter in my life. I arrived happy, innocent and hopeful.

In less than a year, my marriage was over. All my dreams, hopes and expectations had been dashed. Every single day of those months had been humiliating.

When I joined him, I thought I had left behind the torturous seven months in India I had spent with his mother, being constantly nagged and having pretty much everything I did scrutinised and criticised. It was a crazy, disheartening period.

But I was wrong. The time in India only set the stage for more abuse to come. It was always over small things, like not cooking as well as his mother did or not talking to her enough when she came for an extended visit four months after I had arrived.

When it was difficult to find a reason to fight over something I had done, he attacked me for who I was or, better put, was not. I was criticised for not looking Canadian enough. My skin was too dark and in need of bleaching. Not speaking and walking in the "Western way"? Whatever the topic of his hatred, the result was a gradual erosion of my very self.

Somewhere along the line, I realised that he treated me this way because he was struggling with his own identity and low self-esteem. I fought within, asking why he got married in the first place. Who gave him the right to do so when he was failing to face the world? Why me? I started to lose strength, amidst the endless stream of tears and questions.

I was over burdened with domestic work, forced to change my looks and, at the same time, pushed out of the house to look for a job. Don't bother dreaming about finishing your studies, they said; you have to bring in your fair share of money. I struggled to adjust, gave my utmost but could not sustain. My health started to suffer. The combination of being emotionally weakened by his wrath, the distance from India, the cold unfamiliar environment, and having to face the joint insults from him and his mother took a toll.

Faith, family and friends in India kept me going. These are just the initial hiccups of marriage, they comforted. Things will turn for the better, they insisted... and I told myself. It almost looked like they would when his mother left a month later.

Then, one fine evening in November 2009, nine months after my arrival, he deserted me. It was over. Just like that. No sorry, no explanation, no words. No farewell.

I was left standing all alone. A cold and lonely road ahead.

My immediate challenge was to find a shelter. With tears in my eyes and a heavy heart, I approached the local social assistance office for some form of support. Deeply appreciative of the precious money they gave me, I was able to afford the dignity of taking care of the basic needs of food and a roof over my head, in the form of a small basement room.

As the days went by, I was able to look more squarely at the situation at hand. I broke down... many times... not because of how he had treated me but because I had been betrayed of innocence, of love, of honesty. It was a bitter hurt.

However, each time I felt like giving up I would shake it off, telling myself that defeat was not an option; somehow, I had to make it through for my friends, my family and my faith. Through this period, my two siblings gave me unflinching support. I was not able to speak to my parents for a few weeks. I knew that they were shattered and I did not want to upset them further. I leaned on my siblings and steadfastly held on to my faith.

I spoke to my mother a few weeks after. The moment I heard her voice, I felt a composed and powerful force urging me to stand up, and not give up. I knew then that there is no insurmountable hardship. I could not talk for long before losing control, but from that moment on I knew I couldn't afford to be defeated. That was the moment I decided to walk this path with grace and determination.

Fighting him was not important for me; fighting injustice was. He had never looked back, had never asked where or how I was. This relationship was a façade. A mockery of a union of any sort.

The big question was, "Now what?" Should I go back to my parents? Should I fight him in court? Maybe life would be easier if I packed everything and returned to India quietly?

But I did not want to give up quite yet. So, I made a few decisions. I would not fight him for alimony. I would not turn around and run home. I would look for a job where I was and create a meaningful life on my own terms.

I had to be strict with myself, sometimes lovingly, sometimes upfront. My family wanted to visit me, but I refused. Perhaps because somewhere deep inside, I did not want my parents to live in that cramped basement room and go through the life that I was living. I assured them that all would be fine. They, in turn, picked me up each time I faltered, and made sure that I did not give up.

I hunkered down and mounted a job search. Within two months, I joined an environmental non-profit organisation as an intern. Nine months later, I managed to save enough to move to a studio apartment—my royal castle, where I could have peace of mind. Even if it was only furnished with basic pieces from garage sales, I treasured it, and also the friends who helped me get that far—helped me move, helped me clean the apartment, and gave countless encouraging words.

I lived in Canada for another year, during which each day seemed to bring a new battle of divorce papers. Despite the briefness of our marriage, this man could not let me leave without further pain; from taking his sweet time to sign documents to making dirty accusations about my motives and conduct during the marriage. To add insult to injury, this all resulted in a massive legal bill. But, again, each time the slope turned downhill, my faith convinced me of one thing—winter will turn to spring. Determined to clear my past of everything to do with "him", I worked harder, saved every penny and paid the lawyers. Finally, and rather mystically, almost a year to the day that the nightmare had formally begun, the divorce was finalised. My contract with the organisation I had been working with also came to an end. I rejoiced. So, it was time, I decided, to go back to India, to return to my home. Time to see my parents after a year of self-discovery undertaken essentially in solitude. It was time to see how they were doing. To let them see for themselves, and perhaps through that, for me to also cement in my heart and my mind, that I was fine.

I packed up, giving away every item I had gathered—furniture, cutlery, books—to friends, mainly students who were struggling in this new land. The best part was, none of these bonds required us to be related, to be Indians, to be women. We were from different cultures, countries and circumstances. But we were together in our differences, each with hopeful hearts and a desire to reach out to each other on good days and bad. Looking back, I guess what I cherish most is the beautiful ties of friendships formed; a learning that everyone has their struggles; and a certainty that a belief in humanity, together with my faith, meant that I simply could not give up.

On arriving in India, I was welcomed into the warm and comforting arms of my parents and siblings, who stood eagerly at the airport with tears of happiness that I was finally back with them. That we could all "live" again.

Life has had other challenges since. But these I feel are small compared to what I went through in Canada. Since returning to India, I have met so many young women who lament that they are not yet wed. Maybe with the certainty of a sister who has developed wisdom not from age but from experience, I confidently encourage them to wait for the right time and the right person. And there is an inner confidence that, sooner or later, I too, will carve out a new, happy story for myself. I am reminded of a few short lines from a poem by Dr. Daisaku Ikeda:

Though today may be difficult,
Live it with Joy
Convinced that the road to final Victory
will arrive without fail.

• • •

Deepa Hazrati was born and raised in India. She studied Environmental Science and completed her M.Phil degree from Jawaharlal Nehru University, Delhi before moving to Canada. Deepa firmly believes in the philosophy of Human Revolution and hopes to contribute in her own way to world peace and the happiness of those around her, through her work and approach to daily life. Deepa is now working as an environment and development researcher in New Delhi.

EDITORS' NOTE

Searching for Faith

Jing grew up in an environment of tremendous economic success and rapid social change in China. Many children of her generation have been labelled "little emperors" because of the undivided resources and attention they have received at home, a result of China's "One Child" policy. Some have been criticised for their indulgence in material pursuits and excessive consumerism.

Jing's story is interesting because she went in search of something intangible. Jing arrived in Nigeria, a place very different from what she was used to, and ended up with a series of adventures. The journey brought unexpected clarity. In reading this story, we are reminded: never stop asking. Never stop searching. You may have to change your lenses before you are able to see that which is most valuable to you.

Searching for Faith

by Huang Jing

"Nothing which is true or beautiful or good makes complete sense in any immediate context of history; therefore we must be saved by faith. Nothing that is worth doing can be achieved in our lifetime; therefore we must be saved by hope. Nothing we do, however virtuous, can be accomplished alone; therefore we must be saved by love."
– Reinhold Niebuhr

"Here I come, Dark Continent—an unknown world. Will I be able to find the evidence of faith?"
– Huang Jing

The generation of Chinese people born in the 1980s is unique. This is the first generation emerging from China's "One Child" policy. Our formative years were shaped by the first waves of capitalism drowning out communism. It was a time when people moved away from a philosophy of sharing, of accepting the direction of the collective, and became more focused on the individual. Being the centre of attention at home, these so-called "post-80s" people, who are now young adults, have big egos and plenty of self-confidence. Unbound by religious traditions, their preoccupation tends to be material achievement over spiritual and moral cultivation.

I belong to this group, and followed a path typical of my peers—excel academically to get a good job, work hard at a reputable company to obtain a higher salary, and gain social standing and strive to accumulate as many assets as possible to secure a comfortable life. I performed very well in the highly competitive environment into which I was thrust—I attended the best university in China, earned a postgraduate degree from a world-renowned institution in Europe and then, joined a leading global consulting firm.

Despite these early successes, I struggled in my profession, which involved working on complex, long-term issues for which there were no easy solutions. Most times, I was disappointed at being unable to witness immediate impact in the companies we served. Even when project delivery did happen during a relatively short space of time, I was dissatisfied with the direction of it. I ended up frustrated with this seeming inability to bring about effective change quickly.

I came to the realisation that *thinking* through interesting issues alone (and being financially comfortable while doing so) could not sustain me. I needed something more to hold on to, something tangible to rely on, and something that could address the long-standing question in my mind: "What makes life meaningful if life itself is full of expectations and aspirations that can never really be fulfilled?" Religious people carry their faith in the existence of God throughout their lives, facing the sinful world with grace and believing in a better life in the next. What about me? What is my faith?

Upon the expiry of my initial entry-level job contract, I had the opportunity to reconsider career options: to the outside world, the most promising path was to go to business school and rejoin the firm two years later— with more credentials, a higher position, better pay and a clear career trajectory. Ignoring the advice offered by friends and family, I resisted the temptation to pursue a predictable future. Instead, I chose to sign up as a volunteer consultant for a cocoa livelihood programme in West Africa. Perhaps more out of curiosity than a fundamental rejection of consumerism, I decided to explore my response to an environment without any material incentive. Perhaps, I could find what was missing in my life?

Ironically, I was more ignorant than fearful when heading for Nigeria; little did I know that it was, and still is, the largest and probably the most culturally complex country in West Africa, with a reputation for being tough to work in. My introduction to the country was an inauspicious one. Just five minutes prior to the flight landing in the commercial capital of Lagos, the pilot informed us that he could not touch down as there was another plane on the runway. While these "near-misses" happen even in the most advanced of airports, this unfortunate welcome did not bode well for my experience in the country. Not long after, I found myself caught at random roadblocks (in one instance, a group of bandits tried to stop the car with a board of nails in Ibadan), almost hit by a car while walking happily along a busy Lagos street, and told stories of frequent kidnappings (one of my best friends was abducted at gunpoint while working in the East).

Notwithstanding these experiences, there was plenty of time to focus on what I had come to do.

My job was to help local cocoa farmers increase their income through better access to technology, business knowledge and agricultural inputs. After a few weeks of doing field work, I was shocked to learn that instead of re-investing in their land, what most farmers did with their additional income was "buy" more wives, have more kids, and acquire cars and houses (most of the cars being second-hand trash imported from the developed world).

It became clear that having more money did not necessarily mean a better quality of life, especially if effort was not made to change people's mindsets and behaviours. Education was thus crucial. But this is a tricky issue as it requires intensive effort and its impact will only be felt with time, sometimes after many generations. As we see elsewhere in the world, such slow-to-show interventions do not appeal to politicians who are keen on winning the next ballot: for that, the more direct approach of dishing out subsidies—in some places called "t-shirt politics"—to various businesses is more effective and thus preferred.

Much of my work involved creating microfinance products to help farmers gain access to agricultural inputs within a period of five months. But, as the work progressed, I realised that if farmers did not have a credit culture, all risk measures would fall apart. The widely applied collective guarantee approach (for instance, ten farms within a community guaranteeing each other for debt repayment) would also result in collective default.

Contrary to what my well-trained consultant mind would have suggested, the solution to this credit culture problem was not in the design of a financial product with a well-structured profit-and-loss statement, but in the piloting of a simple product amongst a small group of farmers, following up with rigorous tracking and monitoring, and gradually expanding from one group to many. Again, this required a very long-term commitment. A few private companies, including chemical companies and exporters, had been giving farmers credit, and some received positive outcomes only after ten years of experimenting. Not surprisingly, I was once again certain that my task could not be fulfilled within the five month project timeline.

However, the biggest challenge I encountered came from losing trust in people, including those I wanted to help and those I needed help from. I was told lies by seemingly innocent colleagues and counterparts—from house helpers and drivers, to work partners and government officers, and learned that people could be tempted to cheat their family and friends for a pittance. Good intentions were manipulated by the organisation I was working for, who cared more about gaining additional funds and accolades from donor agencies than about empowering their staff and volunteers to assist those in real need, in order to have real impact on the lives of the people they were being paid to help. I was terrified and depressed. The thought of leaving the country well before my contract was up crossed my mind many times.

"When facing many aspects of the heart of darkness, in Africa and the world more broadly, remember the light, and we are the symbol of that light," wrote my friend in an email to me during this time.

Then, things suddenly took a turn for the better: I met two exceptional people. Trevor is a British agronomist in his late sixties, with more than thirty years of experience working in Africa. He leads Adamawa Agricultural Development and Investment Limited (ADDIL), and lives in Yola, a city close to the desert, in the northeast of Nigeria. Yola is a place with a very harsh climate and hardly any modern luxuries. However, I was astonished by the way ADDIL functioned. In contrast to many of the staff in my previous organisation, every employee at ADDIL, including the secretaries, drivers and cooks, arrived at the office before eight in the morning. Secretaries often worked over the weekends, drivers were eager to take the night shift, and cooks would gladly cater to individual preferences. Drinking water was always replenished on time, the projector was always ready before the meeting and people were always willing to help whenever there was a problem.

"Change starts from very small things, and doesn't come by default from the two-thousand-hectare hybrid-maize land one has cultivated or the six-million-dollar-investment chicken farm," Trevor told me. "And you have to be persistent: when I first got here, nothing worked the way it does now; I made things happen—showed people how to do things, and then kept checking as many times as necessary till it was done correctly. It is painful, but you see the change in people, and I believe they can carry these changes home."

I was particularly heartened when, at a birthday celebration for a member of the staff, I overheard Trevor whisper to a guy behind him, "Will you make sure that every driver and guard gets a piece of cake?" He is a role model, not only because of the smart ideas he has brought to a difficult part of the world, but also because of the effort he takes to change the way people work and live. There is no magic for change: just do little things persistently.

Sir Patrick, too, is a legend. He is Nigerian, and has never lived outside the country. He worked at Novartis Nigeria for several decades, going through several organisational changes within the company, before becoming the CEO of Syngenta (currently a legal entity of Novartis), the market leader in the agro-chemical business. After retiring from a stellar career, he started PatenGlobal, an agro-chemical distribution company.

The first time we met, he was quite cynical towards aid organisations and my motivations for being in Nigeria. I shared with him my struggles and told him that I had come here looking for faith. Surprisingly, he appreciated my sincerity and we became good friends.

One day, I asked him why he chose agriculture instead of oil as a career, given that he was from the Delta State, the oil-rich part of the country. He laughed and said: "Young girl, if everyone thought that way, we'd have no hope. My passion is in agriculture, and I believe that I can make a difference by helping the poor gain access to better quality chemicals. Every morning when I wake up, I know what I am striving for. This gives me peace of mind to face the imperfections along the way. I know there are so many problems with this country, but I'm a Nigerian, I will be here for my entire life, and I'm prepared to wait for things to happen."

I was overwhelmed with admiration. Passion and faith, something that both of these men have, are truly powerful drivers in life. With these two things, one can move mountains.

The five months I spent in Nigeria were transitory, and my work seemed trivial compared to all the problems confronting the country. That said, meeting remarkable people like Trevor and Sir Patrick made me realise that however small the effort, it could still make people's lives better. My simple ways of thinking and acting could provide some inspiration to others. I taught the house helper of a friend how to make Chinese food, which in turn encouraged her to open a restaurant; gave candid advice to one of my Nigerian friends looking for a job, and he has now started to make real progress; and fell in love with a person working in the country. We gained tremendous emotional support from each other, making each day easier.

In return, I found my faith: by persisting, I can make a difference to people in need through many little efforts— perhaps no giant leaps, but a contribution nonetheless.

And it doesn't need to happen all at once. Nigeria has taught me much about passion, but also about persistence and patience.

• • •

Huang Jing's life is a tale of multiple cities. Born in Fuzhou in Southern China, she lived in a military courtyard (her father worked for the Army), before moving to Shanghai (Fudan University), then London (London School of Economics) for her university degrees. She worked in Beijing and Frankfurt before embarking on her life changing experience in Akure, Nigeria—this "in the middle of nowhere" place that helped her find her faith in life. She is now working with the Bill and Melinda Gates Foundation China Office. She is constantly looking for inspiration and opportunities to contribute to society and remains excited about her personal journey to find the true meaning of life.

EDITORS' NOTE

Trilogy of Thoughts

While working as a temp at a gas station during my school holidays, a man approached me and asked if I was ruled by my head or my heart. Random setting, random conversation, random question. Perhaps, not so random after all, as I have asked myself the same question over and over for the last twenty years—to rule with my head or my heart?

Selina's trilogy of day and night; dreams and reality; time and life suggests that the answer lies somewhere in between. One cannot be devoid of the other. They complement and make us whole.

Trilogy of Thoughts
by Selina Ho

Between day and night
My soul awakes in the night,
Seized by desires unseen, unknown, unheard,
By the day's eye

Deepest dreams unawares,
Reveals itself in great longing,
In the blackest night

Darkest creatures buried deep,
Rises above the dream-like state,
A spectre in the night
Memories sublime forgotten,
Reign supreme,
In the cloudless night

A sliver of light slashes the sky,
Dawn breaks,
Chasing away the ghosts of the night

The spirit lifts with the light,
The sun putting colours on the land,
And all seems right

As I lay supine pondering,
I wonder what is real,
The day or the night?

Perhaps the truth lies,
Where the soul and spirit meet,
Between day and night

I fly in my dreams
I fly in my dreams,
a gift that lifts the spirit,
and nourishes the parched soul
The desire to reach the sky dwells deep within
Some say we should fly with wings like eagles,
strong, magnificent and proud,
majestic, effortless

Soaring above all else
Soaring is made easy with love bearing the wings,

when paths are straight and steps are light
but life's loss, pain and sorrows,
weigh on the flesh and spirit

Perhaps....

One should fly like the little sparrow,
light and easy, always levitating,
happy in summer and in winter
joyful and free, wings humming...
The song of the sparrow
the flight of the sparrow
and the life of the sparrow
...small but beautiful

The wonder of time
Time is a wondrous thing, I say

It heals all wounds, they say
It encourages, it nourishes, it tolerates

It reveals all things, they say
It permeates, it designates, it cultivates

There is a time for everything, they say
Each in its place, no sooner, no later

Time is fleeting, they say
It comes, it goes, it doesn't stay, seize the day!

A stitch in time saves nine, they say
It prepares, it readies, it prevents

Time is valuable, they say
It is gold, waste not
Time is eternity, they say
It is relentless, with or without us

Time and life walk intimately, I say
As one,

Moving forward, giving hope
A New Year, A New Beginning

• • •

Selina Ho was born in Singapore, where she spent most of her life before moving to Washington, D.C. in 2008, to pursue a Ph.D. degree at Johns Hopkins University. She is currently writing her dissertation. A political scientist by day, Selina writes about and dwells on policy and international relations issues. She writes poetry when inspired. To her, poetry is introspective, emotional and necessary, an integral part of life and inseparable from her being.

EDITORS' NOTE

Transitions

From a young age, Aida's approach to life has been calm, taking challenges, small or big, as opportunities to explore what lies around the corner, not over-planning, but just lettings things unfold.

As a child of mixed heritage, she has also often had to put effort into fitting in. But each challenge, each life transition has been seen as an opportunity to step up her game, work that bit harder, and be that much more creative. The result is proof that, with a healthy dose of optimism and a bit of luck, being different can be a lot of fun!

Transitions

by Aida Axelsson-Bakri

Transition. It has always been about that, for me. My first big transition was taken away from me—literally. They called 7th grade the "transition" year at the International School of Lusaka in Zambia, where I studied. And when I was in 6th grade, the school decided to cancel the "transition" year! Three classes of 6th graders—ninety students—were informed that they would not be coming back in the new school year to "transition". Instead they were to proceed to "Form One", which was 8th grade.

Not a very ceremonious beginning to the series of transitions that would follow in my life. But no matter. Transitions, be they small or big, are central. Transitions are the keys that open up doors to the future. They contain moments from which we can learn so much, and during transitions, we become both wiser and have fun!

By all standards, I was a tad young to be transitioning to university in Belgium, and we all knew it: my parents, my friends and myself. I was embarrassed about my age, to the point of avoiding any questions about it like the plague. Luckily for me, most people never bothered to ask, and had it not been for some "overly helpful" professors who shouted out, "Oh! You're the sixteen-year-old!" for all to hear, I might have gotten away incognito.

Living independently at that age was exciting, but also tough. The bank would not let me open an account on my own, or perform any meaningful financial transactions. I was allowed to withdraw money but only at the counter, certainly not from an ATM, and I could only make transfers with prior parental approval; I guess they didn't consider minors to be fiscally responsible. This was how it was until I was eighteen. And it wasn't just the bank that caused trouble. Getting a phone or cable TV (not that I could afford it anyway) was the same. Prior approval from Dad was compulsory. Come to think of it, I couldn't even get an ID card without someone's signature!

To top it all off, my host family option fell through soon after I started school, and I needed to get my own apartment. I decided to room with the girl who had been standing in front of me in the line when we had been queuing to sign up for the host family programme.

(Her host family's dog was eating her homework, so she decided to room with me instead!) However, the hunt for a place big enough was yet another hurdle for us to overcome.

"Vous avez quelle nationalité? (What is your nationality?)" we would be asked via the parlophone at the door of some of the prospective apartments. "Suisse, et Allemande (Swiss, and German)," we replied in unison, which was true enough—to the extent that we were both "half" these nationalities (the other half being slightly more exotic: in my case, half Ethiopian, the result being a rather olive complexion, brown wavy hair and deep chestnut eyes; in my friend's case, half-Japanese.) The problem was that neither of us resembled the blond-haired, blue-eyed Swiss or German girls that some of the landlords were expecting. This seemed to be such an issue that on a few occasions, we literally had the door slammed in our faces.

To give a flavour of the xenophobia that was (and still is) alive and well in some parts of Europe, our experiences ranged from being "randomly" picked out to be searched for drugs by cops in Gare du Midi, after coming off a late night train, to being denied entry into selected upmarket discothèques. Oh, my circle of very international friends and I have had our share of discrimination and I'm afraid it has had a lot less to do with our (not so) dodgy characters than our "true colours".

But I was young and adaptable. Somehow, I managed to get through this transition from the idyllic International School of Lusaka where at least half my classmates were "half something" to the "real world" of city life in my university years. I learned to brush off the discrimination and not waste time trying to prove ill-doers wrong. We also learned, with the rise of the right wing political parties in some Belgian cities, to be careful not to ruffle too many feathers as our safety could be at stake.

Some years later, I embarked on the unforgiving task of trying to find a job, smack in the middle of a recession. Months went by with hardly any job ads appearing in the papers and, when they did, the competition for these positions was ferocious. For jobs in Brussels, even junior positions, one has to have one to two years' work experience, a master's degree and be able to speak four or more languages. Needless to say it was a daunting prospect.

Then one day, a dear Norwegian friend from university called to ask whether I could step in for her as a receptionist just for one month during the summer. She had planned to work there herself, but had suddenly changed her mind and thought I might be interested. As a Swiss citizen, I was actually the right nationality for a change!

I applied, got the short-term position, and was asked to start immediately. First I had to learn to operate the switchboard. That was fine. Then I had to learn the names of the people who worked a few floors higher up in the building. That was not fine. Not fine at all.

My employer, EFTA, the European Free Trade Association, represents four nations: Iceland, Norway, Switzerland and Liechtenstein. And almost all staff originate from these countries. It was my first contact with Icelandic names, and I had no idea how to pronounce them. In addition to that, the two drivers (a very funny Belgian duo) who hung around the reception when they were not out driving the directors, were of absolutely no help whatsoever.

Half way into my first day, I realised I would not last long if I didn't figure out a way to learn these names fast! How to get the right intonation. How to figure out if they were male or female! I somehow managed to solve one part of these mysterious appellations: if a surname ended with a "dottir", then the person would be, without a doubt, female. If the surname ended with a "son", then the person would be male. However, this only solved part of the problem, and so I stayed up late several nights in a row memorising the pronunciations of the names of my new colleagues! I am fairly certain that this extra effort, silly as it sounds to me now, was key to getting "very good receptionist" status within a very short time!

They asked me to stay another month. And I did. I loved the job, however menial. Then they asked me whether I could cover for one of the secretaries who was going on maternity leave for a few months. I did. They asked me if I would cover for another secretary, and another, until I had finally worked in all the different units of the organisation and got myself a splendid overview of how EFTA worked and the overall European political environment.

But after a year there, one of the heads of unit sat me down and said: "Aida, don't get stuck here. You should move on and find yourself a job related to what you have studied." His words hit me like a lead balloon. I had been perfectly happy at EFTA and the only drawback I could see was that these were temporary positions. But he was right, and for the first time I began to realise that I had the potential to choose what I wanted to do. So, I started searching again.

Soon, I was accepted for a traineeship at the European Commission in the Directorate dealing with Research, and more specifically in the unit dealing with Biotechnology. Although this traineeship did not last long, just a short five months, it was the perfect bridge between EFTA and the consulting jobs that came after it. As a matter of fact, on hindsight, I don't think I could have qualified for my first consulting job if I did not have the experience I had in the Commission.

My first consulting job came unexpectedly. I was having lunch with a friend from EFTA (the only remaining Irish member of the staff) and at that point, I had just finished my traineeship and was, once again, desperately looking for work. The intense search for a job was producing no results and, the best I could hope for was to get a letter saying, "We will keep your CV on file for future reference." On the way out of the EFTA building, I ran into one of my favourite former bosses in the corridor who asked me what my plans were for the future. I said that I was now officially on the job market again and he explained that he was clearing out his office and leaving EFTA to join an EU transport policy consultancy the following week. All that sounded fine and I wished him well in his new endeavours.

As chance would have it, I received a phone call from him that very afternoon during which he told me that the firm he was joining was looking to recruit a junior consultant. And for a full two hours, he proceeded to tell me why I would be perfect for the post. So I applied, interviewed, and within a few days, got myself a new, more-real-than-real job—all thanks to him and the incredible coincidence of our paths crossing at just the right time.

It was a fantastic environment. Small company, highly specialised, experienced bosses, and I learned a lot. I spent three and a half years in that environment and was saddened when the company suffered an unfortunate sequence of events that led serendipitously to me departing and setting up a business, with two other colleagues.

Starting a company in a very heavily-burdened-by-red-tape country like Belgium was no easy task. In fact, I would venture to say that I had to re-encounter a number of earlier life trials to varying degrees during that process. My age (still too young to be taken seriously—at least back then!), my nationality (not being from an EU country), my qualifications (or lack thereof), all came up at one point or another, again and again, as challenges. Not to mention that I had no specialised business skills or training. I learned to think logically, practically, and not put too much emphasis on how things should be but rather on how things are and how I would want things to be. And together, we managed to create a very pleasant and empowering workplace.

Today, I run the company on my own and, together with my colleagues, we provide strategic advice on EU policy. We work on interesting topics that motivate us, and refuse to work on matters that we consider unethical or where we have conflicts of personal or business interest.

I'm truly blessed to be living happily in Belgium with my husband, William, and our two children. William and I went to primary school together and, as friends, skipped the "transition" year together. So it is a very interesting coincidence that he ended up by my side through many of the subsequent transitions I didn't skip. After having left Zambia, we kept in touch by letter (long and detailed accounts of our individual challenges!) and met up again shortly after I completed my first year in Belgium. So I fell lucky-in-love with another mixed kid, bizarrely also Swedish-Ethiopian, who could perfectly understand my being from "nowhere and everywhere" and, together, we chose Belgium as the country we'd put our bags down in for a little while. It just turns out that our "little while" turned into two decades, something that I only recently realised, perhaps because I'd been too busy enjoying the moment!

In truth, I'm grateful every day that a particular individual came along at each of my transitions. They have believed in me and given me a chance at the unlikeliest of times. Taking those chances, believing in those people who believed in me, is what life is all about. Those people are central and those transitions define who you are.

And if we're lucky, it will all just be too good to be true.

• • •

Aida Axelsson-Bakri was born in Ethiopia to a Swiss mother and an Ethiopian father. She grew up in Uganda, Kenya, Zambia, and Nigeria, where her father worked with the UN, before moving at the age of sixteen to study in Brussels. She worked as an EU policy consultant for nearly four years before starting her own consultancy focusing on EU transport, environment, energy and health policy. Aida is married to an Ethiopian-Swede, William, with whom she went to school in Zambia from the age of eight. This truly international couple are now happily rooted in Belgium, where they are raising their two children to be citizens of the world.

EDITORS' NOTE

Work-Life? Balance.

We are able to relate to Elizabeth's story as it deals with one of life's inevitables—the sickness and death of a loved one. In her contribution, Elizabeth shares the memories of her mother in the months leading to her final goodbye. Her writing conveys a sense of grief yet it also comforts. It is comforting because her recollections of her mother are very much how we would like to remember our loved ones who have passed on: how they have been an integral part of our lives and how they will continue to live on in our beings. It is also how many of us would like to be remembered, come our turn to go. As living creatures, we all have to confront the joys and pains in the unending cycle of life and death. The best way to do this is to treasure every relationship and appreciate each moment as is.

Work-Life? Balance.

by Elizabeth Burden

My life changed one night in a dirty ATM booth in New York's Chinatown. I remember getting out of the cab. I remember realising, as my feet hit the sidewalk, that the cab had still been moving when I opened the door and that I hadn't paid the driver. I remember cradling my phone in one hand, heavy and precious. I remember wrestling with the sticky door of the dingy cash machine cubicle, knowing it would be quieter there than the street. I remember the sound of my mother's voice when she told me she was dying.

When I was young my mother always cleaned our house. I thought at the time it was a measure of pride and independence. On hindsight, I think it was a form of punishment for the fact that she was so smart—she had graduated top of her class in college, phi beta kappa, an entire year early, but had never, ever worked. I remember how proud she was of all of us—myself, my two sisters and my brother when we got jobs. Her eyes glowed when we worked during the summer. I made coffee at a local café, earning six dollars an hour. "It doesn't matter," my mother said. "A job is a job. It's important to work." And work we did, all of us. We washed cars and fed dogs, we watered plants, babysat, taught riding, sailing, watched houses, stacked hay—anything at all. Mum never asked us to clean up after meals, to vacuum, to do our own laundry, as if indirectly saying to us that those skills would make us unfit for anything else. "I'm so proud of you," she said, as we trotted off to work at 5am. And to my sisters and I, "You girls are so smart, you can do anything. I could have had a career. I was smart," and with a smile, "Don't be like me."

Every summer, every winter break, from the sound of the last bell till the moment our feet hit the bottom step of the graduation platform, we worked. I realised much later that the only times in my life I had not had a job were during my long stints of travel—carrying a backpack from town to town to see every church, climb every steeple tower, mail postcards and figure out how to book a hostel bed in eight languages. "When are you going to get a job?" my mother asked over the faint echo of the long distance call.

After graduate school I took a job with an energy company and began working as hard as I ever had in my life. When I drove home late at night, the roads empty and foggy, I would call my mother—three time zones behind, and she would say, her voice glowing, "Well, Lizzie, I'm so proud of you." She gathered all of our accomplishments together as if they were hers. I met her friends and they knew every project I'd worked on, every success I'd had, where I'd gone to school, how many countries I'd been in. I felt embarrassed but also secretly special to have my career followed by strangers.

I lived out of take-out containers and suitcases. I had mustard in my fridge, and yogurt that had expired two months before. I had one sponge under the sink gathering dust and three microwave-safe plates from Crate and Barrel. I went home to sleep, to lug back dry cleaning, to collapse into bed, only to awake again, startled out of a dream, my Blackberry flickering next to my head.

"You're such a good businesswoman, Lizzie," said my mother.

On 22 February 2010 my mother was diagnosed with stage four lung cancer. My world slowly turned upside down.

The doctors told us we had two weeks. Then they decided it was maybe a few months. Or maybe not—no one was sure. Without ever discussing it, we all moved home, my sisters, brother and I, slept together in the living room like we used to when the power went out—pulling blankets off the guest beds and piling in front of the fire. Every two hours we all woke up together to bring her medicine. She called us her snow geese, what with the way all four of us flooded into her room silently, stepping unerringly over a squeaky board, streaming into the darkness to kneel by her bed. Each person with a job: one with pills, one with morphine, one with water, one with crackers. We didn't need to go together. We shouldn't have gone together. But the doctors told us that at any moment she could be gone. We didn't want any one of us to find her gone, alone. Two hours of sleep, the fear, the panic, the quiet breath in the dark, the comfort, two hours of sleep.

Repeat.

My father, meanwhile, was at a loss. My parents' marriage existed almost out of time—a holdover from a different generation, when roles were outlined so starkly that the language of flexibility did not even exist between them. My father controlled the perimeter. My mother controlled the centre. They co-existed for almost forty years, content with this balance—like spinning disks, always in harmony, never intersecting. Now we had all moved back and the centre of everything—of dinners and laundry and scheduling and life, was upstairs in bed. The balance had inextricably tilted and he didn't know what to do. He paced around the outside of the house. He tried to help. He took over Mum's morning medicine run at 6am, learning for the first time in his thirty-seven years of marriage where we kept the tea bags.

He would set up the tray the night before, the tiny china tea cup looking ridiculous in his hands, as he set the spoon gingerly into place, always flinching at the clang of spoon on porcelain—and counting out her medicine as carefully as a child trying to catch a leaf frog, his large hands clumsy with the spill of tiny white pills. I ached for his precision, knowing he believed—we all believed—these strange superstitious things that come with grief—that perhaps a perfect breakfast tray makes some kind of a difference. He would leave suddenly in the morning to go to his office. Then return to find all of us working, playing cards, reading to Mum. He would hesitate in the bedroom doorway, rocking on his toes for a moment before remembering some task outside that he had left undone. He gave the impression of a man leaving more rooms than he entered, wandering lost in our own house.

During the day I tried to work, running down my old checklists of emails to answer, things to do, but I faltered. Even during my worst weeks of work—flipping through slides in the conference room as the sun came up, showering in the locker room downstairs before a 9am meeting—I had never been tired like this. Mum slept most of the day, but we could not. As the days went on, she slept more and more—we slept less.

We would dress her in the mornings, a new sweater and lipstick—always lipstick—and she would have a visitor, or the chaplain would come and sit by her bed and read her poems or prayers. We sat with her when there were no visitors, reading to her, telling her stories, asking all the questions we could think of, unwilling to miss a moment. We brought her bright catalogues full of summer fashions and impractical gauzy dresses that existed in some other world where no one was sick and everyone was always five minutes late for a party. Sometimes my sisters and I would go out to buy all the things on the pages she carefully dog-eared, her hands trembling from the medicine. We would never wear them, but they delighted her—the soft warm colours of summer in her hands.

Even when she slept, we hated to leave the house. I prowled around the first floor, the living room, the library, the kitchen, the dining room, around and around and around, so tired I was dizzy. For the first time in my life, work was not an escape, not a refuge. Not a warm place where I belonged and felt needed. I struggled to try harder, to do better, the pressure of letting my team at work down competing with the pressure of letting my mother down—and eventually work submerged under a long, slow slide into panic. Mum was asleep upstairs. There was nowhere to run.

One day, on one of my endless, aimless laps, I noticed the counter in the kitchen was sticky. I looked under the sink. I remembered Mum doing this when I was younger. There was a bottle of something in there. I pulled that out. Clorex. I sprayed it on the counter. Suddenly it smelled like winter evenings when I was young—when the house was warm and sleepy and there was a faint scent of tea from the little porcelain cup and saucer my mother always carried around the house—her cups left on tables and railings, half empty, with the faint impression of lipstick.

I scrubbed all the counter tops. My head felt clearer. I started washing the knobs on the cabinets. I swept the floors. I mopped them with old wax polish from the cleaning closet I'd never opened in my life except to dig for hidden chocolate chips. The bathrooms were disgusting—what with all of us living in the house. I cleaned those. I took the dirty towels to the laundry room. There were stains on one of them from coffee. How do you remove coffee stains? I had never asked Mum that. I ran upstairs to check. I suddenly felt the tiniest bit better. Righting the house seemed to centre something within all of us. Suddenly we all had jobs inside—and at night, to have the kitchen warm and glistening, the beds made, the smell of a fire, gave the impression, however faint, that we could weather the storm.

As my mother got more and more sick, I slowly began to learn all the things she had never taught me. I remembered all the things she loved: lemon scents on antique wood, ironing lavender into a pillow case—crisp and white. Fresh cut strawberries on a plate with a tiny spoonful of honey. How to arrange all the fresh flowers that kept arriving every day, sent by her friends who loved her and whom she was too sick to see. "I always ironed all the pillowcases with lavender, ever since we were married," she confided to me one day. "Your father has no idea."

I tried to go back and forth—to maintain my life in Washington, D.C. and to be in Seattle. Back and forth across the country—back and forth eighteen times—no matter where I was, I was always in the wrong place. At work I worried about Mum so much I couldn't concentrate. I called, I texted compulsively. One day in a meeting I was trying to text her and dropped a cup of coffee on the rug just as a conference call began. I pressed the cheap paper towels into the carpet, ashamed to be in this meeting on my knees, cleaning. I sent Mum a text message—another in a series of conversations about carpet stains—tried to make it funny, asking her what to do. For the first time in my entire life, she didn't respond. The next day I got four texts in a row from her—all gibberish. I called my youngest sister. She said, "Mum is frantically trying to text you. She's convinced you need to get a stain out of the carpet." I went home.

In Seattle, I abandoned all pretence of work. My computer was the only thing in the house allowed to gather dust—sitting quietly on the dining room table, plugged in exactly where I left it, its blue light flickering faintly as the battery slowly drained.

On 27 May at 4am, just as the first birds began to sing, my mother died. The rest of that day my family silently scrubbed our house together for the first time in our lives—wiping baseboards, washing counters, folding laundry, mopping floors—trying to stay ahead of the grief. Trying to imagine how pleased she would be to see the house glistening, a calm centre in a storm of grief.

Since my mother died, I have not been able to find refuge in work the way I always did. I'm not sure I ever will. My work made my mother so proud. But now, when I look back on those years of eighty-hour weeks and business trips, I remember how narrowly my life was focused—surrounded by piles of stacked paper and dust, always more comfortable in my email inbox than in my own life—one step, one task, one presentation ahead of loneliness. I know my mother pushed me to succeed to try to save me from narrowing my horizons—she wanted more for me than to be a housewife, tucked into the tiny orbit of household cleaners and organic vegetables. Strangely enough, I had gone too far the other way, losing myself instead to powerpoint and deadlines. Neglecting friendships, neglecting space for me to be anything else other than being good at my job.

I know how much my mother loved me and how much she wanted me to succeed, but one of the final gifts she gave me, how beautiful and unexpected, was the gift of balance. In the end, she taught me how to make space for myself to grieve, how to build a shelter from the storm instead of merely hiding from it in my work. She also taught me how to remember her. Now, the smell of lavender and ripe sweet strawberries, crisp clean ironed sheets and hot black tea bring my mother back to me, and make me feel as if she could be standing right behind me. She would, I think, be surprised to find that these last things she taught me have been the ones I needed most; talismans against the brutal, the menacing, the unexpected blows of living—a balm for grief and a place to breathe away from the storm.

Now I hope very much, if my mother looks down on me, that she is not disappointed to find out that I'm quite a lot like her after all.

• • •

Elizabeth Burden was born in Seattle, but spent most of her formative years on San Juan Island in Washington State. She studied Economics at Smith College, after which she took a position at the Weatherhead Center for International Affairs at Harvard University. Elizabeth has always fought very hard against becoming an author, no doubt a leftover habit from her mother who wanted her to concentrate on making a living. She currently works with the International Finance Corporation on Resource Efficiency, while writing on the side. Elizabeth lives in Washington D.C. with her partner, Rachel.

EDITORS' NOTE

Three Women in My Life

Maya's story speaks of the inspiring influences in her life—a ballet teacher, her mother and a public figure. Coming from a small village in Japan, she could easily have been confined by the small-minded expectations of the people around her. Instead, she succeeded in spreading her wings to experience the world and contribute her skills and talents at a broader level.

Maya's story reminds us of the teachers in our lives for whom we can be thankful because they influence, guide and inspire us to reach beyond what we dare to contemplate on our own.

Three Women in My Life
by Maya Horii

Although I did not appreciate this until I was fairly grown up, my family was more externally-oriented and internationally-minded than the average family in Japan. My father, a typical "salary man", was a civil engineer and spent much of his professional life in the 1970s and 1980s working in the Middle East and Southeast Asia; it was a time when Japanese construction companies were leading many new development projects of ports and harbours around the world.

My mother stayed home to care of my brother and I, but nonetheless had a small global experience of her own— she taught Japanese in a language school to students from abroad and befriended American, European and Asian scholars who were visiting the university in our town. At least once a year, she invited students and friends to our home, delighting visitors with homemade food, putting the girls in kimonos and taking dozens of photographs of everyone.

And so it was that I grew up curious about the outside world. At my elementary school graduation, every child gave an almost obligatory one-sentence statement after receiving his diploma. Most asserted things like, "I will work hard in English and Math classes when I start middle school" or "I will make a lot of friends in the new middle school I'm attending." I remember saying, "I want to make a difference in the world by working internationally and helping people."

My first exposure to someone with experience in seeing the world (other than my father) was my ballet teacher, Yoko Ichino, who came to our studio for the summer and winter as a guest instructor. I was about ten years old then. Yoko and her husband, David Nixon, were principal dancers at the National Ballet of Canada at that time, and appeared as guest artists in Europe and America. (Today, they are the Ballet Mistress and the Artistic Director of the Northern Ballet Theatre in England).

Yoko-sensei taught our ballet classes; Nixon-san choreographed pieces for our summer recitals. I practised English ceaselessly so that I could talk to them. Yoko was always bursting with energy and had an endearing smile. She demanded a lot from her students, but was also surprisingly positive and encouraging. As far as I can remember, that was the first time in my life that I had received so much affirmation. Because of Yoko, I learned to love working hard and was happy to be in the upbeat environment of our ballet class all day long in the heat of summer.

One day, after several hours of rehearsals, Yoko showed us a video of students at the National Ballet School in Canada performing the exact same piece that she and Nixon had choreographed for us the previous summer. As I saw the beautiful, blonde, tall and slim girls perform the piece that we had thought was ours, tears began to roll down my cheeks uncontrollably. Mixed emotions of jealousy, envy and a realisation that I was never going to be good enough overwhelmed me. Yoko pulled me aside and told me, "If you believe in what you are passionate about, and you love what you do, it doesn't matter where you come from and what you look like. I know you dance with your heart, and that is what's important." These words from a world-class ballerina have made me focus on what I am passionate about to this day.

By the time I started high school, I became increasingly frustrated by the fact that even though Japan was ranked the world's second largest economy (at least, until recently), our leaders, both in the political and business arenas, had very little presence on the global stage. Japanese companies—Toyota, Sony and Nintendo, to name a few—may be well known around the world, but no single manager at or near their helm appeared charismatic or influential enough to stand head-to-head with other global leaders. I concluded that this was the result of a largely passive and reactive education system that focused on rote learning and did not cultivate a student's ability to problem-solve, communicate and express himself, especially in English.

When I was seventeen, motivated by a drive to see the world outside of Tokyo, I left home for a year on an exchange programme, to live with a French-American family in California. This was my first time in America and life was full of new discoveries. At the same time, I grew to better appreciate the surroundings in Japan—public transportation that allowed me to go everywhere on my own, and the almost universal service hospitality of stores and restaurants. After returning home and finishing high school, I received an offer to attend both the University of Tokyo, one of the most prestigious schools in Japan, and Harvard University in America. I ended up spending five months at the University of Tokyo after high school graduation in March, meeting many friends and even joining the cheerleading squad, before leaving for Harvard in the Fall of 1998.

While I was a third year student at Harvard, my professor of Japanese Politics introduced me to Dr. Sadako Ogata, then the United Nations High Commissioner for Refugees, at a dinner that honoured her accomplishments within the organisation. Dr. Ogata became the agency's Head in 1991, and handled various crises, from human rights issues in Kosovo to Rwandan refugee camps. A small, soft-spoken Japanese woman, yet quietly determined and strong, she gained respect from people around the world for tackling the most difficult challenges of her time—saving the lives of millions of refugees while maintaining neutrality amidst the conflicts and evolving political events.

Her conviction and humour made me feel that she could singularly pave the way for our generation. Dr. Ogata said to me, "You have already accomplished so much to be able to study at Harvard, and there is endless opportunity ahead of you. You should try anything you want to do, without being scared of what mistakes you would make or what others would think of you." That became my second mantra.

After college, I found my passion while working in Indonesia and the Philippines. I had my first direct exposure to the world of foreign aid, often witnessing first-hand how things did not work, especially due to the lack of capability and attention to project management. I decided to pursue a degree in economic development at the Kennedy School of Government to better understand the workings of government. Together with sixty-five other classmates representing more than twenty-five countries, I had the unique opportunity to learn from friends from all over the world, and immerse myself in the study of international development.

As the end of the programme approached, there was the question of what I would do afterwards. My mother very much wanted me to pursue a Ph.D. She had been supporting me all these years through my obsession with ballet, my decision to participate in an exchange programme, and my leaving home for college. In some sense, I think she lived part of her own dreams through the freedom that I had. In return, I have always tried to live up to her expectations and be a good daughter—to do well in everything, from school to ballet to other after-school lessons.

As a professor without a doctorate, my mother knew more than anyone else how having a complete set of credentials was key in the male-dominated world of academia. While it is true that my mother managed to successfully secure a university teaching position for herself, eventually heading up a department for Japanese language instruction, she always felt she could have achieved more had she furthered her education.

I thought hard about the decision—despite my mother's advice, my love for working with people and making tangible changes to their lives did not seem consistent with spending another few years in research to pursue a Ph.D. I wrote my mother a long email to explain. It was serendipitous that, just as I hit the "send" button, a note arrived from her—it read: "Do what you would like to do, life only happens once, and it is yours to make it what you want it to be—don't think of what I want you to do."

There are still many things I would like to accomplish—I want to have a big family, live in Africa, not only work as a consultant advising others but also run my own organisation—but I am very excited about the path ahead and I cannot thank these three women enough: a graceful ballerina, a committed humanitarian, a patient mother. Each so very different yet equally influential.

I'm still trying to figure out how to make a real difference in this world. But I feel fortunate enough to have these mentors who have continuously told me that there is no limit to what I can do, so long as there is a will and passion, and so long as I'm not afraid to make mistakes. Every now and then, I still take the easy path forward when confronted with choices, but I'm hopeful that my teachers' influence will push me closer to pursuing my dreams.

• • •

Maya Horii is a Japanese native who decided at a young age to spread her wings globally. She found the first opportunity to travel abroad at the age of seventeen and never looked back. Maya has a penchant for positively impacting the lives of others and is constantly looking for ways to get involved in development work, particularly within Africa. Maya recently relocated to Washington D.C. with her husband and baby son Kyle so that she can better pursue her passion for international development.

EDITORS' NOTE

Finds on a Beach

Can the super woman have her cake, cookies and cream, and eat them all? A career that provides income and status and also a true sense of contribution; a house with the smell of home cooking meandering through the rooms on a Saturday afternoon; kids who have their runny noses cleaned and all other needs taken care of; friends and family showered with her presence and love; "the romance" with her man fuelled conscientiously, all while keeping her simple makeup and hair in place and adorning fashion that makes a bold statement?

What happens, if in the midst of managing her multiple life-stakeholders, fulfilling roles and responsibilities—and busily stacking up more new "to do"s in that mental notebook while she sleeps, like a super-efficient back-office—she forgets how she feels and what she wants? Obligations. Expectations. Happiness. Others. Ours. Mine. Very often, we confuse ourselves. Sometimes, we lose our way. Fortunately, we can also find it again.

Finds on a Beach
by Lena Brahme

Some time ago, I chanced upon an episode of the programme *The Search for Happiness* on Swedish television. It was mentioned in passing that, while Swedes obsess about "finding themselves", Americans decide "who they want to be", then try to achieve it.

I am a thirty-six-year-old mother of two, who, amidst a fulfilling life of "must do"s, has somehow lost touch with who she is and what she wants to be.

The summer and fall had been arduous. The loss of my mother, termination of a work contract and move to a new home had left me frayed along the edges. When an old friend suggested that we take a long weekend off to the south of Spain, I jumped at the opportunity. Every part of my being yearned for a "time out" from daily chores. January pitched up, surprisingly cold even for the season, and my husband, children and mother-in-law bade me farewell.

We travelled to the small town of Estepona along the coast and stayed at a hotel that was right on the beach. Temperatures ranged from twelve to nineteen degrees Centigrade and the weather was ever changing—sun and rain, taking turns. It was tranquil and lazy. We had sleep-ins and late nights with red wine and reminisces. Gradually I felt my pulse coming down.

However, even with the gentle breathing and yoga stretches, a sense of hollowness dwelled within. It wasn't the longing for my family. I did miss them and actually relished the opportunity of missing them, knowing full well that I would soon see them again.

Rather, the void, I realised, was me missing me.

I had arrived at one of those forks in life where one had to decide what to do and which way to go. I tried listening to my inner voice for guidance and found, to my dismay, that it had gone silent. What did I want? Not just for my family but also for myself? Who did I want to be? In Sweden these days, what you do and who you are seemed inextricably interlinked. Being out of employment had made me feel less of a person. So easy and convenient it is to be swept up in a routine where satisfying the demands on the job and meeting the needs of others take precedence over one's own.

I found myself all alone on the stony beach one morning while taking a stroll, and started entertaining one of my favourite pastimes—searching for "what-not"s: one never knows what one may find swept up on a beach, especially after a long windy night. I walked, head bowed low and slowly worked my way north. Now and again I stopped for a shell or a stone of varying colour or shape. I have never ceased to be fascinated by how these curiosities can have such lustre while lying wet on the sand, only to become a dull non-descript greyish white object when placed on a mantelpiece, with the smoothness of its surface barely hinting at its origin. Perhaps, it is an act of cruelty to remove something from its rightful place where it is able to shine in its original glory?

As I strolled along the beach, it suddenly occurred to me that this wasn't just any beach. I was in Spain! Surely I ought to take a moment to savour the beauty of the surroundings, and not remain fixated on what's on the ground? I raised my head and let my eyes gaze over the waters. The Mediterranean lay perfectly quiet, the sky a husky grey with stripes of radiant white licking the horizon. Somewhere on the other side lay Africa, a broad backbone, sensed but rarely seen. The stillness and beauty at that point in time contrasted vividly and starkly with my everyday world. How many times have I allowed beautiful scenes such as these to pass by in oblivion as I rush to complete errands?

Plonking myself on the shore, I hunched forward to hug my knees. The bubbly waterfront interlaced with sticks, seaweed and the odd plastic scrap. Shards of building materials and shells had combined to look like a carpet rolled out. Here and there pieces of ceramic tiles could be seen. Being in Andalusia, where floors and walls are customarily clad in beautiful ornamental tiles in homage to the Moorish past, I decided to add pieces of decorated tiles to my list of "what-not"s to pick. Many pieces I saw were monochrome, having had their vibrant colour eroded by the sun, waves and sand. Only the vivid red ceramic stood out, keeping some of its hue. When we strip ourselves of our outer décor, what remains?

I came to a sudden halt. Having been lost in my thoughts for a while, I had nearly walked right over the body of a fish. A dead fish. Must have been left behind when the tide receded. It was large, nearly a metre long, shaped almost like an eel but with a long back fin sweeping like a ridge from its head all the way back to its tail. The mouth ajar, no sharp teeth nor anything scary visible. There was no smell, only the salt-scented sea air. Once a formidable lance in the water, it now lay dead on a stony beach.

I looked around, had anyone else seen it? So ugly, so exposed, so cold... so sad. We all end up like that. Be it in a fancy coffin or somewhere altogether different. And here perhaps was the lesson of the dead fish: we all die, doesn't really matter how, what matters is how we have lived. To the fullest of our abilities or sleep-walking on autopilot, following the routines of every day. Surely living is the lesson? I backed away from the sea creature with as much respect as I could muster.

Looking ahead a few hundred metres, I saw an old tower, withered by the centuries. As I approached, I saw a lone scuba diver slowly make his way into the water, a bright orange floating contraption in one hand and what looked like a harpoon in the other. Standing thigh high in the water, he let go of the orange floater, revealing a thin chord which linked it to himself. Slowly, after having crossed himself repeatedly, the diver kissed his fingertips, leaned back and descended into the water. Such solitude. Who did he rely on for safety? I shuddered at the thought of having to get myself wet in the event the orange floater disappeared below the surface.

Letting go of control, relying on one's own abilities or the gracious assistance of others—these are difficult things to do, I thought, but why? I realised that I was in many ways letting the fear of failure hamper my existence and decisions. I looked out to the sea. I could still see the orange floater in the distance.

Something beckoned from the ground beside me and broke my stride. I hunched low. It looked like the inside of an oyster: a mother of pearl gleaming rich and wet. The shell was perfectly round with a rugged and thin vertical edge all around. Gingerly, I picked it up by its side and turned it over. It was the bottom of a metallic can. Something had turned the inside into a feast of beauty while the outside merely signalled junk. I gently returned it to its soft perching place. If this old discarded can could regard itself as an oyster full of mother of pearl, why shouldn't I consider myself a treasure, regardless of whether anyone took notice?

Rolling back onto my feet and standing up, I caught a full gust of wind blowing straight into my face. In the distance I could see dark clouds rolling, preparing to offload some of their burdens. I started to trot back home. A small stone in an almost amber shade caught my eye and I picked it up. As I did, I dropped two shells. At this point both my hands were full of stones and shells. I wondered if I was being gluttonous, trying to gather everything that had caught my fancy.

Maybe I have to sort through my catch and drop one in order to take another, I thought. Prioritising has never been my strong suit and I laughed as I tried to balance my pirate's booty more carefully to allow a final acquisition. Maybe that too is an art I need to muster? To learn what to keep and what to discard. To learn to say "no" to some offers and "yes" to others.

In adulthood, time had become such a scarce commodity. Especially time for nurturing the self. I had equated the yearning for such time as being selfish. There'll be plenty of future opportunities—when the kids are older or when someone else's needs have been catered for. If they are happy, I am happy. However, have I carried this axiom to the extreme? If I don't fill up my own well every now and again, the well will run dry. I must allow myself to be happy.

Thank you, I breathed to no one in particular; the beach, the morning, the approaching rainfall. As I raised the little amber pebble from the ground, a ruffle swept through the drying seaweed around it and there, a jolly neighbour, lay a perfect shard of Moorish mosaic.

· · ·

Lena Brahme is the daughter of a Zambian mother and Swedish father, who grew up steeped in both cultures, though one was much more prevalent than the other at different times in her life. Over the years, she has tried to find that oh-so-delicate balance between being an independent woman, a loving partner, a good friend always ready to laugh or comfort (depending on the occasion) and, now, added to the mix, a good mother. An architect, she studied at Lund University and lives with her husband, Lars, and two young daughters, Malou and Smilla in Malmö, Sweden.

EDITORS' NOTE

The World is Perfect

This contribution reminds us of our younger days, when we were always game to try something new, always looking on the bright side of things no matter what happened. No doubt, this is a good attitude and the right attitude to carry through life. Yet many of us are all too easily jaded, losing our youthful zest in the daily tumble. Too often, we let life slip into a trudge and become a chore.

Xiao's contribution speaks of the simple beauty of life, surrounding us with ideas familiar and comforting, leaving us refreshed to confront the day's vicissitudes. Truly, youth is a function of the state of our mind, and not the body. Steer with the rhythm of life, savour its sweetness and do not be afraid to venture into the unknown.

The World is Perfect

by Xiao Yu

There are many things about the future I am not sure of. After all, life has already taken several surprising turns. Many a time, things have not turned out the way I expected.

One of the surprises was the choice of what degree I should pursue at university, the single biggest occupation of many Asian parents. Like all parents, Asian parents want the best for their children, though the "best" can sometimes be defined in the narrowest possible sense.

When the time came to make my decision, all my dream career choices—computer game programming, anime or movie producer, novel writer—did not pass my parents' reality checklist and were flatly rejected. Instead, they wanted me to pursue a specialised field and offered me a choice between the more lucrative and respectable career options of bio-chemistry, medicine and law. It was at this time that my grandparents stumbled upon a local newspaper article, listing some of the most popular career choices. They picked one and called my parents (though they later admitted that they had little idea what the job entailed; they only thought the title sounded cool). My dad took to the idea and decided it was a good fit. I thus ended up studying Actuarial Science.

Looking back, this was probably one of the best "non-decisions" I have ever made. I am very happy with the way things have worked out. My best friend, Qiong, who chose to study Chinese Literature and become a professor and writer, is equally happy. Sometimes I wonder if my life would have been like hers if that newspaper article had not fallen into my grandparents' hands.

Qiong and I have known each other since we were three years old. We are like sisters, so close that she calls my dad "Dad" too. Till we entered university, our paths had been very similar—we had very good grades and everyone we knew had high expectations of us. Under family and societal pressures, Qiong enrolled to study International Economics and Accounting in one of the best universities in Shanghai. But in her second year, she took up another major in Chinese Literature and graduated with two degrees. Certainly not an underachiever!

While most of her classmates went searching for their "pot of gold" in multinational companies, Qiong ditched the "big plan" and went on to pursue a Masters, then a Ph.D. in Chinese Literature. Qiong always had a passion for Chinese Literature so I was not surprised by her decision. Rather, I was impressed by her courage to pursue what she had always wanted to do. Most people regard writing as an unstable career and very few parents would wish their top-of-the-class only child to go into that field.

I have no doubt that Qiong will become a highly regarded professor in her field, doing a job she dearly loves and enjoys. But like everything else in life, there is a trade-off. At the moment, Qiong worries about her daily expenses and the high rental costs in Shanghai, given her low salary as a teaching assistant.

Like the old saying goes, you win some and you lose some—it is difficult to have everything in life. Despite our common interests and achievements, Qiong and I ended up with divergent career paths. The bottom line is: we are both content with our decisions. What we do not have reminds us of how lucky we are to have what we do have.

Life is not an equation with one single right solution. It's more like a poem—as long as it sounds right to you, then it is a good poem, even if it does not make sense to others.

When I was twenty, I met a friend who changed the course of my university life. Minnie was two years older than I, and was my statistics tutor. We shared the same boarding school experience, were both studying Actuarial Science, had the same drive to be good at what we did, and coincidentally, even shared the same family name.

Minnie and I became good friends very quickly. Even though we stayed in the same city for only a short period of time before she moved back to Hong Kong, I learned a great deal from her. Most importantly, Minnie showed me the impact one person could make and how the action of one could have repercussions on many others.

In my second year of university, I applied for a tutoring position. These positions were normally only open to more senior students, so I was a little surprised when I was accepted. During a conversation later on, the professor mentioned that he had an "exceptionally good" tutor who was also a Chinese girl—Minnie. She tutored in many courses and was doing exceptionally well. At that instant, it occurred to me that the reason I had been accepted for the position was probably because of Minnie—the good work she had done, and the positive impression she had made on the professor. Through her exemplary contributions, Minnie had paved the way forward for me and probably for other Chinese female students too.

This incident made me realise that sometimes, one's deeds affect not only oneself but others, including people we may never meet or know. I have since resolved to do the same for others—to always be considerate of the consequences of my actions and to contribute to make the whole larger than when I first found it.

As depicted by Dickens, life can be dramatic. Three years ago, life presented me with both "the worst of times" and "the best of times". I had a back injury that took me more than three months to recover from. I was completely incapacitated and could not drive, work or even cook. All I could do was stay in bed and watch movies, and I was getting more and more upset over all the important tasks that I was unable to do.

Life took a turn when I read a quotation, "The world is perfect, you just need to be damaged enough to see it". Strangely enough I started to see the perfections embodied in the world around us—the privilege of being able to walk without pain, the blessing of being able to sit in front of my computer, even the joy of being able to work hard to rush for a deadline.

I started to notice the little things that I had never thought about before: the love of my family, who asked me to return home to China so that I could get some rest, the support from my finance master supervisor, who granted me a long leave of absence from work so that I need not stress about anything, the kindness of my colleague who gave me rides to the office whenever I absolutely needed to give lectures.

I saw that many of the things that I was obsessed about, like making sure I did not fail exams or make mistakes at work, were in fact so insignificant. None of them actually mattered in the end. What really matters is health, family and friends. What really matters is that I am still alive, I will get better, things will get better, and the world is perfect.

Sadly, as I got better, I started to worry about the "insignificant" things again. In fact, they are not totally insignificant: work, money, achievements. After all, they are what make me who I am. It is a small thing, perhaps, but as a way of not falling back into taking life for granted, I have designed an opening screen on my cellphone that says, "The world is perfect, so am I"—to remind myself to treasure what is important, to remind myself that I must appreciate even the small day-to-day things I can do, such as walking and breathing without pain.

Talking about the surprises in life, I am hopeful that there will be many more to come. I would like to travel the world, work in different countries, learn different practices in the actuarial field, and get exposure to all aspects of business. One day I would like to go back to China, maybe build an actuarial consulting firm of my own, and work on education initiatives to grow local talents in fields relating to finance, risk management, investment and insurance. Well, truth be told, part of me would also like to retire early and go back to writing, painting, drawing, or to become an anime or manga producer.

Who knows what will happen in ten years, twenty years, and beyond? I think despite how much we think it through and plan ahead, we will never fully comprehend the future consequences of the decisions we make today. But as long as we are still alive, the pains, the mistakes and the surprises all make us a better version of ourselves. After all, the world is perfect. We just need to put the right lenses on to see it.

· · ·

Xiao Yu was born in Harbin, northern China. She currently works in Johannesburg as a Consulting Actuary and plans to gain experience in various countries before eventually settling down back in China. Although Xiao Yu chose the tried and tested path of actuarial science, she continues to pursue her creative instincts in her spare time. She writes fan fiction, reads and draws manga, and harbours plans to retire into the make-believe world in the long-term.

EDITORS' NOTE

Girl Powerful

The powerpuff girls were a hit not too long ago—sassy figures using superpowers to fight villains. With their direct and sometimes brutal approach to defending justice and other beliefs, they quickly became role models for aspiring young girls. Louise reminds us of a powerpuff girl. Her eyes open wide when she speaks about her latest adventure at a project in Mozambique. Frown lines on her forehead deepen markedly when she reflects on the frustrations of getting water to people in Lesotho.

However, like many of us, Louise also struggles with finding her place in the working world where not everyone lives by the same rules. Is the answer to conform and get things done without fuss, or is the better way to keep "girl power" alive and take others to a time when life had fewer qualms?

Girl Powerful

by Louise Croneborg

My Skype rings loud and clear: "Do-do-dong-do". Those rounded buttons appear, interrupting me from staring into the depths of my laptop. I press the green button: "Answer with video" and lean back in my chair feeling a smile creep across my face. The top of a small face and bright blond messy hair emerges in front of me. The girl's eyes settle just above the edge of the screen, piercing my heart.

Let me introduce her to you: this is Siri, my niece, my goddaughter, my friend and, most importantly, my source of endless love. Siri is four years old and wants to tell me that she is now drawing a mouth on Hello Kitty as someone forgot to give her one and wasn't that rude? I couldn't agree more.

An incomprehensible collection of reports gloomily

awaits attention on my laptop. But the reports cannot come close to competing with the importance of the missing mouth of a cartoon cat. My sister, Ulrica, Siri's mother, pops her head into the video's line of sight, says a quick hello and then interrupts the cat mouth story; she wants to recount to me the conversation she had earlier in the day with Siri over a glass of juice.

Siri: "Mum, do you know that I'm the one who decides at daycare?"

Mum, looking up: "Oh really, is that so?"

Siri, more determined: "Yes, and Mum, at home... I'm the one who decides."

Mum: "Well, dear Siri... I don't think..."

Siri, interrupting: "You see Mum, one day, in the world, I will be the one who decides."

I wonder what happens to Girl Power when we grow up. Why don't I see more of that wonderful force in my female colleagues, friends and yes, in myself? That fantastic sense of self-awareness, pride and conviction that I am capable of everything and that nothing is impossible. Where did that go? Did it go out of fashion along with rah-rah skirts?

Girl Power is so delightfully encapsulated in Siri's assertion. And that same Girl Power was undeniable in my friends and I when we were growing up; so much so that it seemed to pound along with the beat of my heart.

But somewhere and somehow over the past thirty years, the indestructible, don't-mess-with-me, I'm-it Girl Power just stood up and walked away. Almost as if frightened into exile as the growing young woman shapes up and sharpens herself to fit into a predefined mould.

Girls realise very early on that there is glory in being glorious. "You look so pretty, you dance so well, you smile so lovely, you are sweeter than honey!" And isn't it wonderful that girls are all that? Oh, I can't tell you how I treasure the moments when my Siri and her sister dance around and sing songs about trolls and snails and lambs.

But the flipside of all the praise is of course that girls realise that if someone tells them they aren't all that— then, what are they? Are they girls at all?

A boy at school once told me that I wasn't as pretty as his other girlfriend. He meant no harm! This kid just had lots of... links in his chain, lots of cookies in his jar, or whatever it's called when men start "collecting". Naturally, the only sensible reaction to this judgment was that Girl Power came to the rescue: I told him straight that there was no way he could say such a stupid thing to me!? I gave him a proper smack in the face, turned on my heel, and walked away smiling at the world, knowing full well that he was wrong and that I was clearly amazing.

I'm lying of course. Because, truthfully, Girl Power

never came to my rescue. In reaction to his more-than-jailworthy misdemeanour, my head drooped just a little and I shrugged back in silence with a scar deeper and more painful than I ever would have thought possible.

Girl Power was running for the hills.

When we get older, we have to work. The rules of work are invisible and hard to understand. Yet, by default, we adapt and conform so as not to cause disruption. Girls in particular are great at conforming—I have no idea when we learn to conform and how, but we do. Not to say that boys don't. But for some reason women are exceptional at it.

I ask you, why is there so much conforming in the office and so little Girl Power in the boardroom? And don't get me wrong, I'm not saying we need the likes of Keli or Lady Gaga to blast into our staff meetings and shake up the discussion on budget allocations. I'm just saying that far too many women I know have trouble telling the world what they believe in. So very often, we keep quiet to keep face.

A close friend of mine once went to a life coach for some guidance. When life coaches are good, they provide a sanity check that enable you to attack the tribulations that would otherwise have kept you stuck in the middle of a crossroad. My friend was concerned about conforming and spoke about the sacrifices she made when she let her hard work and professional contributions slip away unnoticed, reducing herself to a silent worker-bee because she's just like the other team players, helping out in the bigger scheme of things. Haven't we all been there?

My friend reflected: "I've worked my little ass off on weekends and late evenings to complete a task, a report, an event, an analysis... just so that someone else can take all the glory?"

In response, the life coach wisely asked, "Why do harm to yourself in order to do no harm to others?"

I want to invent a little bell that gently starts ringing when that happens (ideally chiming Beyoncé's "Single Ladies"). A reminder to say, "Hey, are you gonna let someone shine without you squeezing in to claim some of it, all to keep the office peace? Coz, overall darling, the result is not peaceful! The result is you going home, glum as a wet cat, feeling decidedly uneasy. Unhappy. Unappreciated. Unloved. Yet you have a choice to make here—you are not powerless."

For me, the realisation means that, each day, I try to do three things. I make a choice. I tell the world what I want. And I muster the guts to make it happen. Even if that means falling on my face.

We often think that we are in situations where there are no alternatives. We're stuck, un-free and tied. Whether it's worrying about the status of our pension fund when we should be drifting into blissful sleep, or working at our desks until 9pm on a Friday night when we could be out dancing. Then again, something got us into those situations. We make choices to be there despite doing it on autopilot.

My wish is that when my magic bell rings, there's that split second of exhilarating freedom in our minds that allows for new choices. Say something. Do something. Anything!

When my niece tells her mum that she will rule the world, no one doubts her. There's something about putting words to your choices and dreams that take them from being half-baked to actually happening. It's like closing a door in order to tell the draft to calm down, then opening another door and continuing on your way with the wind in your sails. How else can the world know what you really feel, dream, want and think if you don't express it? And honestly, if you do tell it like it is then there's that chance it might happen. And, even if someone tells you otherwise, it is still worth the try and, for that, I salute you.

In order to make tough choices, and to articulate what it is we want and what it is we don't want, we need to stand our ground. We need to be brave and courageous, and truly believe in our power to achieve our desires. We need to pledge to ourselves and to each other that we will try, even if it is to take the tiniest of steps forward.

And before we know it, Girl Powerful will jump out from hiding and run to catch up with us because this ride is too good to miss.

• • •

Louise Croneborg is Swedish, though of the international variety. Born in Stockholm, she has lived, worked and loved in Spain, UK, Pakistan and Sweden. In 2009, she upped sticks and relocated to Washington D.C. She is a Water Resources Management Specialist with the World Bank, focusing on southern Africa.

EDITORS' NOTE

Unexpected

Life is like poker: sometimes, you are dealt a strong hand, and at other times, a weak one. While poker is in large part a game of luck, on balance, everyone has a fair chance of emerging the winner.

Elena strikes many as a person who leads the perfect life—she is smart, beautiful, talented. This poem is particularly touching because it is about a poker round during which she is dealt a bad hand. Elena reminds us that however wonderful it looks from the surface, there is no need to covet another person's seat at the table because we will all have our fair share of ups and downs.

Unexpected

by Elena Chong

I often find myself placing my hand
Over my chest with rushed anxiety
Trying to tune out the noise around me
Pushing out the swelling emotion in me
To feel my heart beat against my hand.

I close my eyes and follow its beat
Trying to silence the growing panic
Hoping to hear an even beat
Without random pauses or sudden skips
Like the ones I've felt before.

Like the ones that I've felt before
Through my husband's tapping hand
His heavy head on my chest
His other hand gripping mine

Each time my heart skipped a beat or two
Lest a cry of disbelief
May wake the babies who are fast asleep.

Like the ones that I've seen before
Through the monitor above my head
As the numbers shot up rapidly
The nurse's smile turned into a frown
As he rolled in the crash cart by my side
"Just in case" was what he said
With a forced smile on his face
The same expression my husband had
When he told me "things will be fine".

I force out a sigh.

I close my eyes as I lower my hand
That was placed on my beating chest
Breathing deeply as I search my mind
For things to drive out this growing fear.

The softness and warmth of my babies' heads
One on each side of my face.
The unwavering rhythmic beat of my husband's heart
So reassuring to hear in his arms.
The generosity my dear friends have always shown
Whenever I felt helpless and alone.

The breadth of possibilities I have in front of me
As someone who was given a second chance.
I tell myself as I open my eyes
Still blurry from the welling tears
Good and bad things will even out in life
For every unexpected disappointment and fear
There will be unexpected opportunities and joy.

• • •

A Korean, **Elena Chong** was diagnosed with a heart disorder in 2009, six days after she gave birth to her twins. After a three month long bed rest towards the end of her pregnancy due to pre-term labour signs (not uncommon in the pregnancy of twins), Elena was blessed to deliver the two healthy babies full-term. Bringing the newborns home for the first time was one of the most exhilarating moments of her life. However, this joy was short-lived as that same night, she was overtaken by fits of coughing that would not stop. Telling her husband she probably needed a prescription for her cough, she went to the emergency room at 2am, leaving the newborns at home. Little did she know what was coming.

After undergoing a series of tests for over thirty-six hours, the doctors gave her the diagnosis: mitral valve stenosis caused by rheumatic fever. The cardiologist who delivered this news to her by her hospital bed happened to be a mother of young children. She ended her sentence with: "It's a miracle... I can't believe you had twins and are still here... It's a miracle..." Four months later, with only a scare or two in between, she went through successful heart surgery. Since then, thanks to her improved heart, Elena has picked up running. Now more mindful of "listening to her heart", Elena balances motherhood while working at a non-profit organisation in the education sector. She lives with her husband, son and daughter in San Francisco, USA.

EDITORS' NOTE

Two Lives, One Choice

As a sign of our globalised world, there are two contributions in this book about long distance relationships. Both women end up taking risks for love. This contribution is both a reflection on difficult decisions and a light-hearted read of life as an adventure, led one day at a time.

Agga is a determined woman, but she is easy to be with and decidedly natural in almost every interaction, be it a chat with girlfriends or, in this case, trying to "figure it all out" with the man she loves. Agga's life is a work in progress and certainly not without its complexities. But it is also sufficiently positive to inspire us to look at relationships as a journey that should delight and uplift. And, you'll agree, this journey is deserving of a happy ending.

Two Lives, One Choice

by Agga Jonak

What does a girl do when she falls in love with an amazing man living on the other side of the world? What if this man is five years her junior? And how would the answer be different if he is a gorgeous Brazilian whom she met while on a one month beach and jungle vacation? Does she pack her bags, leave home and chase love? Or does she choose the safer option—fantasise, but stay put in a life laid out along the happy lines of wonderful friends, a loving family, and a society which works perfectly (according to many)? And what if this involves a thirty-plus woman who is a planner, incredibly independent, and not one to follow any man anywhere?

At the age of three, she had already decided that she would take a big trip around the world, and even thoughtfully asked Mum to pack a basket of food for her on the road in case she got hungry. She had planned to be away for a while. By the age of seven, she knew that she wanted to have a career that would give her enough money to explore the world, dress like a star and eat well—Italian style? The relationship part, meeting a man and marrying him, was secondary. First create your own stable life, then worry about love.

When she was in first grade, someone asked her class, "So, kids, where will you be in the year 2000 when you are twenty-two years old?" Everybody answered that they would have a family by that time. Her response was, "I'll have a good job and maybe a boyfriend." Apart from finding out that university didn't quite end and work-life didn't quite begin at twenty-two, the rest held pretty well; a happy life and maybe... a boyfriend.

Well, she and her Brazilian man tried the long-distance option, travelling across the Atlantic to see each other every few months, talking daily and sending each other cute little emails to share their happiness in between. What are the prospects of doing this forever? Not particularly great. When other couples cry out of anger, or fight face to face, this couple cried when they walked away from each other's arms at the airport, knowing that once again the marvels of technology would replace human touch until they were reunited again.

So finally, after a year-and-a-half of travelling back and forth and kissing the computer screen good night, the woman, the planner, i.e., I decided to travel across the thousands of miles of water that separated me from this irresistible love.

Yes, it reads like a cheesy romance novel, but I did it! I decided to go to the tall man in Rio de Janeiro, the man with whom I had, in reality, only spent a brief amount of real time when we shared short breaks together. I sublet my apartment to a total stranger, which was in itself a big decision. I took time off from work (five months to be exact), effectively putting my career on ice. All to see whether happiness could actually be lived day by day, every day.

So here I am in a café in Ipanema, taking a break from my ordinary life—living and loving in this cidade maravilhosa. The only covered shoes I have are made for the gym. The only jacket a thin denim thing for the odd chilly night. The only trousers a pair of flimsy leggings bought on a trip to Tokyo some years ago. Definitely a world of difference from Sweden in the wardrobe department, where looking tip-top was what I strove for— freshly blown-out hair, impeccable make-up, and clothes that followed the latest trends to a tee. Where you would very rarely see me in a T-shirt! Or slippers.

It is different here; my loved ones are not around. Every evening, instead of having a cup of tea at a friend's house to ward off the Southern Swedish damp, I go to the beach with my new pals. Instead of sitting on a friend's balcony in a winter jacket, rubbing my gloves together, covered with a quilt while eating French cheese, drinking wine and watching her smoke, I eat acai berries (yes, they work!) and go to the gym with my boyfriend, cursing that it is too hot to work out in sneakers and wondering how I can do so in flip flops instead.

As it was always in "the plan" to learn a Latin language before entering into the afterlife, I decided to make the most of my time here and take Portuguese classes. I have made progress. Three months ago I could only order a beer, thank the invariably tanned and toned waiter for it, and ask for the bill. Now I can have a small conversation with the waiter, understand what he is saying about the weather and wish him a great day at work. Most days, I am filled with the happy rush of understanding more and better, other days I am frustrated to see the language written everywhere, to hear people speak it on the bus, in the waiting line at the supermarket and at the gym and yet not be able to comprehend it all. It is not easy to learn a new language at thirty-two. But it is really so much fun.

It is interesting how a person is able to adapt to his

or her surroundings so quickly and easily. I found it surprisingly pain-free to transition from being fairly well put-together on a daily basis—getting dolled up for work, primping a bit before nipping to the supermarket around the corner, and even wearing lipstick to the gym (yes, I am one of those girls)—to being all natural. Except for some mascara on a big occasion. It is a little more strange to go from being all dressed up for work and driving my car along the highway to power walking along the beach and heading to class in my sneakers and toting a backpack. The last time I used a backpack was in the 1980s.

Perhaps the human ability to adjust and adapt is an inbuilt survival instinct? For me, Rio feels so normal now. I don't even think of the business trips with their fancy hotels, nor the paycheck in the mail every month.

My everyday concerns are no longer about how to make a critical telecommunications device project more efficient or how to make that project leverage the series of complicated engineering processes. Instead, my preoccupations are now more trivial and humdrum, yet no less complicated. Which beach to go to after class? What flavour juice to drink under the hot sun? Whether to squirt on an SPF 30 or 50 (when I never used to go beyond an SPF 4). I spend inordinate amounts of time deciding whether or not to wear that adorable purple bikini.

Laughable, you say? True. But still complicated.

Undoubtedly, this is a short break from my real life duties. This sugar coated break was something I needed, something that both of us needed. We had to make a decision and a choice about love. We simply could not continue to live in a dreamland where neither of us knew what each other was like, or up to, on a daily basis. We had to live through "the mundane", like a normal couple. And then decide.

The good news is that reality is great. Those months sharing a small space in a hot country worked out better than expected. Now, more complications. What is the right decision when two people bring each other so much happiness and, yet each also loves their own homes that happen to be four thousand miles apart? What makes sense when both people also have their hearts where their family and friends are? Is it fair to say that one person should make a "sacrifice" for the other, or is this a word that is too heavy to use in love matters? People I've met here say, "Well you will make new friends wherever you move." Maybe, they don't have my friends.

How much do you give to a man who has the kindest of spirits and treats you in ways that you have never been treated before—who makes you laugh until you cry; who makes the best fresh lime juice in the world; who gives you the warmest hugs every morning and has the most beautiful eyes on Earth? What if he were to make this "sacrifice" for me? Would I, as a result, be indebted to him for the rest of my life? Would it just be a matter of time before he came to resent me for it?

On the other hand, could I and should I take that risky step and move to Rio—for good? Hey, it could be great! Living in a city with such beautiful people, cool beaches and electrifying music year round. A city that is, at this point in time, filled with optimism and opportunity. Full of interesting companies, both big and small, and brimming with talented, free-spirited people—an emerging market in so many ways.

Why is the choice not that straightforward? Have I become that engrained in my ways before hitting mid-life? Maybe I am just one of those people who gets way too attached to family and friends for my own good, not able to let them go to create something of my own. Could I accept being "the aunt in Brazil who brings presents home once a year"? Would it hurt if my friends referred to me as "the pal they used to have so much fun with when they were younger, but now only catch up with once in a while by phone"? Or would all this not matter in a few years, when friends start their own families and spend time keeping their heads above water while managing the daily school run in rainy Sweden and looking forward to summer vacations in Thailand with the kids?

I don't want it not to matter. I really don't want to be the always tanned and (maybe someday rubber injected?) aunt from Rio who shows up every second Christmas with Havaianas flip flops in the latest colours for everybody. But if the tall man from Rio asked me to, I would give it a try.

• • •

Agnieszka Jonak was born in Poland, but moved with her parents to Malmö in the south of Sweden at the age of five. With her eternal tan, unwavering interest in style, and decade-long fascination with Brazilian Jiu Jitsu, many have a hard time believing that Agga is a Computer Engineer, often mistaking her for the happy-go-lucky Team Assistant instead. For ninety percent of the year, she is a Project Manager, travelling the world for business. While she wouldn't dream of leaving Sweden for good despite the winter chill, during her vacation time, Agga scours the globe for lazy palm trees on beaches that stretch to the horizon, where she is equally at home.

EDITORS' NOTE

Breaking Out of the Mould

Melissa hails from an upper middle class English family. Young, well-educated and successful, the path she has ahead of her was well trodden and promising. This story talks about her first foray into the unknown, the setbacks and her reflections.

Initially, Melissa was hesitant to write as she was afraid her story would not be interesting or inspirational. The good news is that words are powerful. Any story, when told from a personal perspective, can tug unexpectedly at someone's heartstrings. Authenticity is often the best source of inspiration. For those amongst us who may similarly struggle with stepping out of our comfort zones, Melissa's contribution might just tip you over the balance.

Breaking Out of the Mould
by Melissa Morris

My whole life, I have had no worries about money or security. I was sent to a top British all-girls' school (away from male distractions), primed to secure a place at a top university, trained to attract job offers from top companies offering top salaries and, after a few years, prepared for entry into a top US business school— all funded by a good employer, of course. By the age of twenty-one, I had two investment banking internships on my CV, a first class honours degree and a position at one of the world's most prestigious management consultancies.

Was I successful? Yes. But was I happy? Not really.

You see, all the years of "success" had boxed me in and made me incredibly risk averse. I had never really sacrificed anything and had taken much for granted. Despite all that I had, I was marinating in discontent.

After two decades of British upper middle class predictability, I decided to break out; to step off the treadmill, much to the cacophony of certain family members and colleagues. In August 2010, I made the bold decision to start my own company—Network Locum—an instant "matchmaking" service that brings together GP practices and locum doctors looking for work. I knew it wouldn't be easy to leave the comfort and security of a well-paid corporate job, but even then, I was not prepared for the roller coaster ride that the past two years have turned out to be.

After twelve months of leaving my "superwoman" career behind, Network Locum was still a baby yet to be born. I had used up all the money I had to start a company and had been rejected countless times by potential seed investors. Presenting my "great idea" to frowning faces was intolerably disheartening. And being (un)fortunate enough to look all of about eighteen years old didn't help either. No longer could I rely on a corporate brand name on my employer's business card to give me authority. I had to learn new ways of being heard. The worst, however, was yet to be.

With money running out, I found myself on a self-enforced starvation diet for a week, in order to have enough money to pay my web developer's wages. That is something I never thought I would have to do!

I had promised customers that the site would be complete by September 2011, but by that date, only a quarter of the product had been completed. After a bit of a spat about wrongly setting my expectations, I had to let my expensive developer go. With no money to pay anyone new, and only a fraction of the product created, I was in despair. The next four months saw no progress. How depressing, and also embarrassing, as customers were persistently asking, "Can we use it now?" I was about to give up.

The turning point came when I joined a Startup Leadership Programme. Networking was the last thing on my mind in my dejected state, but I had to pull myself together and make a concerted effort to expand my network. I found myself enjoying the programme, mixing with fellow entrepreneurs, who were going through growing pains similar to mine. Surprisingly I even made some lifelong friends, and it was one of these friends that took pity on me and introduced me to his web developer friend, James. James completely saved my sanity and my business idea. He agreed to take some shares in the business, work cash-free and complete the website. He believed in the concept and was willing to do evenings and weekends to get it finished. We also had similar ideas about where to take the business and more importantly, were both willing to sacrifice to make it a success.

We are now in a position to launch the website. Looking back, the experience has shown me that with will, conviction and some luck, it can be done.

If I were to give advice to any first time founders, it would be that people are the most important part; who you employ and who you surround yourself with to give you a helping hand when it all goes wrong!

When I first left my job in London to start my web business, I had been pretty naïve to the world of entrepreneurship. Despite the fact that I had been working at one of the most prestigious management consultancies in the world, I certainly had a lot to learn when it came to running my own business. I have been humbled and have learned a lot of valuable lessons since going it alone. There are things I am pleased I did and things I regret. I have so far had more failures than successes. The good news is that I have found what I was searching for—a life less mundane than the treadmill. And I am happy.

• • •

Melissa Morris, twenty-five years old and from England, is the CEO and Founder of Network Locum, an online job matching tool where temporary doctors (locums) can find jobs in General Practitioners' practices, and medical centres, instead of going through an agent. The site went live in early 2012, two years after she embarked on her bold venture. Melissa dreams of being a serial entrepreneur and of being inspirational enough to write for the second edition of this book!

EDITORS' NOTE

A Delicate Freedom

We learn, as babies, how to interact and socialise by role modelling our elders. In turn, our elders guide and discipline us to become healthy, happy and well-adjusted members of society. What happens then, if our childhood is void of role models whom we can look up to and learn from? Aletta's story is about her father and his domineering influence on her life. It is about his inability to loosen his grip and accept his loss of control as he aged, thus stifling ordinary family life for Aletta and the rest of her family. Aletta regains her freedom with his death, though the process of coming out of a shell that has encumbered her for decades remains delicate. We are comforted by the thought that her recovery process has begun.

A Delicate Freedom
by Aletta Jones

To tell you about my life, I must first tell you about my mother. She drove like the devil was on her tail and cooked like an angel. The youngest of five, and the only girl, she left home in the late 1950s to escape a domineering mother who believed that a girl's role in life was to stay by her aging parents' side as a faithful companion, and not much more.

Arriving in London in the 1960s, she wasn't cool or fashionable. I doubt she wore mini skirts or did drugs like her peers. But she was a strong woman who carved out a successful career behind the scenes in politics.

My mother ascribed a small part of this success to her absolute refusal to learn to type, swearing that any woman who mastered the typewriter in those days would be consigned to the typing pool and never heard from again.

As a consequence she forbade my sister and I from taking typing lessons at school. I am to this day at best a two-fingered typist.

My mother met my father in 1972 and, having fallen deeply in love with him, married him a short three months later. I was born three years later, while my sister Alex followed in 1978. My father was thirty-three years older than Mum, but he was a very successful man, full of wisdom and he told the most enchanting stories. So, at first, this age gap did not matter; indeed, it may have been part of the initial attraction. All was wonderful in their cozy little world.

It wasn't until I was six that my father's age began to take a toll on family life. He had been a very fit man in his youth but, as he aged, he went from boundless independence to being incapable of dressing and, at times, even feeding himself. His frustration expressed itself in angry outbursts at the three of us—my mother, sister and I.

His age and sickliness dominated our lives, casting a long shadow over everything. My memory of this time is filled with odd little horrifying moments such as the day my period started. Daddy fell over in the shower and as I ran out of the bathroom exclaiming that I was "bleeding from my bottom" (I was seven years old and as yet the facts of life had not been explained to me), my mother rushed past saying, "So is your father," as she ran to call for an ambulance. It wasn't until the next day at school when a girl one year my senior noticed, and explained everything.

As I got older, I began to resent my father's domination. Perhaps sensing that he was losing control of other aspects of his life, he felt a desperate need to keep us close at all times. I think he knew that this behaviour was unreasonable but, rather than tempering it, he tightened his grip, limiting almost every aspect of our lives in such a way that we could not, if the thought ever crossed our minds, find a way to leave him. This started early on, I suppose. Although fiercely independent, my mother had given up work as soon as they married. From then on, he controlled the money; it was his money, so those who benefited from it had to follow his rules.

The rules stated that he must never be left alone; one of us had to be at home with him—always. He would only permit one shopping trip per week and as my sister loved shopping far more than I did, I usually stayed behind. Some years, I could go for seven or eight months without seeing more than the inside of our house and going to school. We rarely had visitors, even from our extended family. He found putting on an act for them—pretending to be a reasonable, tolerant and indulgent father, rather than the domestic dictator he was—to be a tremendous strain.

Our garden was a fairly large one, about an acre. This was too big. Ideally he wanted to see us, but not hear us. We were expected to play (in complete silence) in the room he was in. Over time, my sister and I became rather accomplished mimes. Twenty years on, we can still convey whole sentences to each other with one look. Our friends find this extremely disconcerting.

Mummy, who had had an almost chocolate box childhood, knew how wrong our lives were and, with the collusion of friends, family and neighbours, she would occasionally get us days out of the house. These days were like a sparkling oasis in the desert. I didn't understand it at the time, often blaming her for being part of the problem, but I see now that she did what she could to help her girls, and to keep the peace. There was no one to offer her such escapades.

It wasn't until a day very near the end of my father's life that I fully realised that my mother was wholly on our side. Daddy and I were sitting in the living room together; Mum and Alex were out grocery shopping. He woke suddenly, desperate for the lavatory. At this time he was using a walking frame to get about and was fairly slow. Unfortunately his bowels could not wait for him to reach the seat and to speak plainly, he crapped on the lavatory floor.

He immediately began to shout for me. As I ran barefoot past the front door I noticed my mother's pale blue Volvo easing into the garage at the top of the driveway. I halted in the open doorway of the lavatory. The stench was appalling and I felt something soft and warm insinuating itself between my toes. I looked down and was aghast.

My father, whom I now realise was only lashing out in shame, began shouting at me to stop dithering and get him cleaned up. The lavatory was a tiny room and, as neither of us was exactly small, I simply could not wedge myself between him and the wall to fix the mess, nor were my arms long enough to reach over him. All the while my mind was screaming, "I have shit between my toes, I have shit between my toes."

In his frustration he became increasingly furious, yelling at my floundering dismay. I began to cry. The more he screamed, the harder I sobbed.

It was into this scene that my twelve-year-old sister walked. She calmly pulled me out of the way and slid in beside him, wiped his bottom, cleaned up the floor and fetched him clean clothes. My mother, who had been a minute or two behind her, found me balancing on my heels (trying not to soil the hall carpet) and watching my sister. I was all but hysterical. As long as I live I will never forget the words my mother uttered when I was eventually calm enough to understand her: "This won't last forever and I will make it up to you."

He was dead within the year and I was utterly bereft. He had been so much a part of our being that I didn't know how to exist without him. Those last few years of his life had seen his health fluctuate so greatly that, even though I knew everyone died one day, I wasn't a hundred per cent sure my father would.

At the same time, his death thrust us into a world of hitherto unthinkable possibilities. We had decisions to make about who we were and what we wanted to be, choices that we were wholly ill-equipped to make.

For almost two decades we had, for all intents and purposes, been his prisoners.

I knew that school would end eventually and, while my friends planned their futures, I didn't imagine for one moment that I would be allowed to go to university. I had never given a moment's thought to what I wanted to do with my life beyond my family and the immediate surroundings of my home.

The journey from my father's death to where and who I am now has been a long and bumpy one. Frankly, you can't emerge from an experience like that without the odd quirk. One of the most noticeable to my friends was my total mistrust and, for some years, hatred of the outdoors. I suppose all those years spent at his side had made me fear the outside world—it was too free and too erratic. I did not know my role in it. The rules were new and elusive, and very different from the controlled but predictable world that I had grown up in.

For years, if there was any chance that I would be outside for a prolonged period of time, I would sit for hours beforehand studying maps of the place, trying diligently to commit to memory any landmark that might help me find the safety of the car or the route home. I was terrified of being lost. I used to write myself reassuring notes and often carried hand drawn maps that I had copied from the atlas or the A to Z in my handbag in case I got separated from friends or colleagues.

It wasn't until I was twenty-five that I began to get over this fear. I had acquired a personal trainer at my gym who very quickly grew bored of our daily regime and decided that brisk walks around town might be a better use of our time. I can't tell you with what dread and fear I set off on a walk with him that first day. I was too cowardly to convey that the very idea of walking in an area that I had not studied for hours made me sick to the stomach. I think he knew there was something wrong, but in the way of all good trainers, he ignored my procrastinations and hesitations and stubbornly persisted. It took a few months of these walks to make me less anxious. As time passed, I began to see that there was in fact no reason to be afraid. I didn't need to be confined to be safe. I'd be fine on my own.

It's too much to say that I am wholly cured. While I no longer loath or fear the outdoors, I still do not understand the impulse to go for a walk. I never need a breath of fresh air, and would happily live out the rest of my life inside the house, never feeling the worse for it. I do realise that I am the odd one out. Occasionally, I take myself out for walks in the grounds of country houses near where I live and wonder to myself if other people around me know that I am play-acting at being normal. I'll eat a little picnic and pretend that this is just how I would spend every sunny day when given the chance.

Inside, however, it's another story. I often feel like a child playing a grown-up; wearing her mother's much-too-large high heels and walking about with a face covered in badly applied make-up.

Speaking of mothers, mine made good on her promise. She snuck me out of school to see my favourite rock band, complimented the choice of colour when I dyed my hair blue, and paved the way for me to make my life what it is today; filled with joy, new friendships and, most importantly, a delicate but precious freedom.

• • •

Aletta Jones was born and raised in the south of England. She studied design and works for a heritage charity which she adores with every fibre of her being. She is currently obsessed with baking and likes to create fantasies with her cakes, never making the same one twice (unless begged nicely). Aletta has dedicated her life to the pursuit of joy.

EDITORS' NOTE

On My Own Terms

Lifelong careers are increasingly rare these days. Many of us can look forward to changing professional paths three or more times within a lifetime. This phenomena is a reflection of opportunities that our parents may not have had, as well as a desire to apply our talents and experiences in different and creative ways.

Towani's story will inspire those who stand at the cusp of a life change but hesitate to make the move, perhaps out of fear that a dream might turn out to be little more than a flight of fantasy. With thick, dark clouds looming overhead, Towani chose to search within and ask herself what she really wanted and how she could live on her own terms.

And, true to the origins of her Tumbuka name, which means "to be so bright and beautiful that you dazzle", the clouds dispersed, allowing sunlight to shine brightly through.

On My Own Terms

by Towani Clarke

I was outnumbered. Three men in suits—Partners—on one side of the room and me, alone, on the other. "We are not asking you to go. Despite the global recession, your job is secure," the Managing Partner reassured me across the boardroom table. "We just want to know whether you are going to renew your contract as Operations Manager," another chipped in.

Four years ago, I had joined the firm as a business consultant to help its rapidly growing operations become more efficient. The first year at the firm was a lifeline in more ways than one. A month before arriving, I had walked out of my marriage of eleven years with little more than a suitcase of clothes and two children to educate, feed and raise. The consultancy work kept me sane, taking my mind off the sorry state of my marriage and wondering what I was going to do with the rest of my life.

Towards the end of the year, I was making significantly fewer trips to the bathroom to cry my eyes out—my way of getting over the break up. I counted my blessings for being a woman and therefore being able to cover up the puffy pink eyelids with strategically-applied make-up. Crucially, the work meant I was able to set up a new home for the kids and myself in Lusaka. It was clear from their father's behaviour that there would be little, if any, financial help coming from him.

After a year, I accepted the full-time position as operations manager to implement many of my own proposed systems and effectively head the support side of the business. I loved working there. I looked up to the Managing Partner who had started the business from scratch ten years before; and had nurtured it to become a nationally and internationally recognised company. Over the last three years, the firm had grown by fifty per cent. I had mistakenly thought I would grow with it.

Instead, here I was, trying to find a response to the question: "Are you going to renew your contract as Operations Manager?" But what new words could I find that I hadn't already used: "I do want to stay but I don't want to do the exact same job with the same salary. I want to progress in my career while staying here. There are still a number of projects I would like to see through, you see."

No words came out of my mouth. The tension built as three pairs of eyes stared at me. No matter how hard I tried to hold them back, tears welled up in my eyes, broke the banks of my lower eyelids and tumbled down my cheeks.

Will anything I say be taken seriously? I thought to myself. It was too late to take the tears back. When I did speak, my voice quivered with emotion. That Friday afternoon I left the office sullen as the depressing truth sunk in—I had put my heart and soul into the job but there was no future for me here.

In the evening, I sat in front of my altar and chanted my universal mantra—Nam-myoho-renge-kyo. I had become a Buddhist almost nineteen years earlier, stumbling across Nichiren Shoshu Buddhism through a friend. This was a religion that made sense to me, was logical and was in line with the laws of physics. The Buddhist Law of cause and effect resonated with Newton's Law: for every action there is an equal and opposite reaction. The equivalent of God was Energy, which was everywhere and in everything, with everybody having an equal part in it. Buddhist practice over the years had helped me through seemingly insurmountable challenges, not least of which was a divorce.

That evening, my chanting was interspersed with outbursts of anger, alternating with sobs of despair. Anger at the Partners for not having had the same vision for the management of the firm or my role in it. Despair, as it dawned on me that I could not allow myself to plateau and stagnate in my career for another three years. I would probably have to leave the place and people I had become attached to.

I kept chanting, working the emotions out of myself, until eventually a calmness came over me. With more chanting, the calmness gave way to gratitude. Gratitude for having a well paying job during one of the most difficult times in my life. Gratitude to have worked with a great team of people and to have the challenges of improving the operations of the Firm. Gratitude to the Partners for not meeting my expectations and hence prompting me to think and feel more deeply about what I wanted to do with my professional life. As I continued to chant, things became ever clearer. I realised that, as much as I enjoyed it and was hesitant of making a move into the unknown, this was not what I envisioned for the future of my professional life.

In my heart I knew I was an entrepreneur. Perhaps I was the grandchild who had inherited the entrepreneurial spirit of our fiery, freckled, red-headed grandmother. During the year between secondary school and university

I started what became a thriving ice cream making business, delivering delights to several big supermarkets. Unfortunately, the business died when I got married and left the city to stay in a small farming town.

Yet that entrepreneurial drive never left me. Even though I was in the middle of nowhere on the farm, I was always growing this or making that to sell. I knew that I would never be at peace with myself until I started and grew something on my own. This was after all why I had chosen to do an MBA instead of my initial choice of a Masters in Horticulture, which would have led me into academia. I spent the year after my MBA working on a business plan for my grand food processing idea. I had planned my life around my marriage and the farm. Naturally, everything I did or planned to do had to fit into the paradigm of the farm, including any business I started.

When my marriage collapsed, it felt like a rug had been pulled from right beneath my feet. Without the compass of the farm and the marriage to base my life decisions on, I didn't know which direction to go. There was no choice but to confront the question I had been avoiding for years: what did I really want to do? Not just what was convenient to do.

When the clouds cleared from my emotional storm, I started to focus on what I truly wanted and tried to distract myself from the lingering disappointment that the firm had not shared my vision for my role. It was at this point in time that the floodgates opened and my ideas began to flow fast and furious.

New Year's resolutions are an important part of my personal end-of-year-cum-beginning-of-year ceremony. In the last days of December, I dusted off a list of resolutions stashed away somewhere in the shelves under my altar. Every now and again I would dare myself to write down a resolution that I might have no clue how to achieve.

For the last two years my resolutions centred around setting up a clothes brand, Kutowa Designs. I was already designing clothes for my sisters and I, usually from the amazing pieces of African fabric Mum brought back from her travels. Strangers would stop to compliment us on our outfits and ask where we had bought them.

That night, I realised Kutowa was my true business baby—waiting to be born. She was waiting for me to believe in her, to give her my time and energy to grow and nurture her.

Then another infant sprang from the shadows and refused to be ignored. Her name was Kuthuta Yoga, Kuthuta in Tumbuka means "to breath". I had started doing yoga regularly almost a year earlier, mainly because

I could do it at home on the living room carpet, which allowed me to spend more time with the kids. Before long, I was hooked. Each day, the first thing I wanted when I got home was to do my yoga. More than helping me stay fit, yoga was helping me heal.

Six months earlier, my yoga teacher had asked me to be one of the stand-in teachers as she was going away. While I did not attend her classes regularly, I took up her offer, very much encouraged by her faith in me. After several coaching sessions from her, I started teaching classes and was surprised at how much I enjoyed them. Like Kutowa, Kuthuta also wanted me to breathe life into her.

Never being an either-or person, I couldn't see why there had to be a choice. Do both, Towani! Do both Kutowa and Kuthuta. Did life always have to be this or that, white or black, right or wrong? Besides, I was a product of two worlds, two colours, two cultures—the child of a white European father and a black African mother. A marriage of defiance against the racism and scepticism from both sides: "Why do you want to marry a native? Is it easy to get a divorce over there?" or "We have just gotten independence from the British and now you want to go and marry one! And you choose a broke one?" and finally, "Think of the children..." Thankfully, there was one voice that blessed the marriage—that of Agogo (grandparent in Tumbuka), my maternal grandmother.

Agogo got her revenge by having fun naming the grandchildren, reminding people of their earlier dissent. In response to the comment "Think of the children" she named me, the first of the four children, "Towani" from the root word "Kutowa" meaning "so bright and beautiful you dazzle". It was her way of saying, "Don't worry about the children. They will be bright and beautiful," and "As you can see, this union (that you earlier rejected) is also beautiful."

Kutowa Designs had in her DNA some of that defiance and confidence, that something beautiful can come through the clash of differences, of contrast, of the merger of divergent worlds. Kuthuta was born from the attempt to handle the stress that usually arises from the clash of two worlds. Like the tension from comments that came from my mum's fellow university students, "She just married him for the money. Just look at her driving his car." Or the confusion, when Mrs. Clarke turned up for an appointment and she wasn't white.

Mum turned to the relaxing breathing exercises of yoga to calm her nerves, ease her insomnia and stop her from snapping at her one ally—Dad. During her pregnancy with me, she did yoga and as a young girl I remember joining her on the sitting room floor as we tried to contort our bodies to imitate the figures in the book placed in front of us.

At the end of the evening, after conversing mentally and emotionally with Kutowa and Kuthuta, I was ecstatic. I knew that to be true to myself I would have to leave the cushy and secure job at the law firm to give full life to my business babies. I prayed that I would make enough for myself and my two human babies to live a decent life.

Two years after that life changing revelation, my businesses are growing steadfastly.

Kuthuta Yoga is a little bigger than her sister. In 2009, I trained in Cape Town to be a certified yoga instructor and have been teaching ever since. Kuthuta has seen almost two hundred students pass through her doors, and has a slowly but surely growing following. There is even a Facebook group following my weekly yoga blogs. Kuthuta is ensuring that me and my now not so small children are comfortable.

Kutowa is the smaller sister, though she has it in her stars to shine much brighter. In the last two years she has released five lines of clothing, has appeared in a couple of local magazines, a local and regional website, and has taken part in four Zambian fashion shows, including representing Zambia at a regional fashion competition and winning the award for Most Creative Designer in the Zambia Fashion & Designers Awards 2011!

It is interesting how one's view of a situation can change. One moment you're in tears, wondering how life could have gone so wrong, how a marriage you based your life on could vapourise; how a job that you so loved and were devoted to could have no room for your further growth. The next minute, you feel immense gratitude for the unmet expectations that had appeared once-so-important but are no longer when viewed on hindsight. To life, for pushing you out of your comfort zone. To the universe, for allowing what comes so naturally to blossom, rather than to remain silent and sheltered in the shadows of your heart.

The pain and loss, the searching and questioning, the late night pondering on life's next steps has led me to put my destiny in my own hands.

• • •

Towani Clarke was born in Zambia to a Zambian mother and English father. The eldest of four children, she grew up surrounded by academics, freedom fighters and women's activists. Always the dutiful daughter, she was perhaps expected (or expected herself) to follow one of these paths. Instead, Towani became a farmer. She has since continued to carve her own path, balancing the many things that matter to her—spirituality through yoga, creativity through fashion design and, of course, motherhood. Towani lives in Lusaka with her two children.

EDITORS' NOTE

The Choice to be Grateful

This is a book of multiple blessings. We find blessings in the stories of love and happiness shared and in knowing that one is never alone in times of pain. Embedded in each contribution is the important truth that these stories are personal and unique to the author but also universal in the experiences that many of us have gone through, are going through and may go through at some point in the future. Zeryn's story is a wonderful way to conclude this journey. We wanted to end on a positive note, with the first axioms we learn as children—to count our blessings, one by one. In the hustle and bustle of living, it is often easy to overlook the gloves that fit and be distracted by the itch on the little finger. Learning to be grateful takes us to the realm of contentment where one can smile and be at peace even when the water in the tap runs out, because we remember that the power is still running and we have light in the house.

The Choice to be Grateful

by Zeryn Mackwani Sarpangal

"There is so much about my fate that I cannot control, but other things do fall under my jurisdiction. I can decide how I spend my time, whom I interact with, whom I share my body and life and money and energy with. I can select what I eat and read and study. I can choose how I'm going to regard unfortunate circumstances in my life— whether I will see them as curses or opportunities. I can choose my words and the tone of voice in which I speak to others. And most of all, I can choose my thoughts."
—Elizabeth Gilbert

"Gratitude is the memory of the heart."
—Jean Baptiste Massieu

I made an explicit choice a few years ago to give thanks daily. This simple and almost trite practice of being grateful for all aspects of my life has slowly changed the lens with which I see things. It has helped me see beauty in little things throughout the day, appreciate the deeper meaning of everyday occurrences, and seek opportunity in challenges (though not before I have taken a couple of deep breaths).

So here are the types of things on my daily gratitude list:

- A cup of morning coffee—the taste and smell are truly some of the best parts of waking up (though mine is not always Folgers—for those who have heard the jingle).

- Quiet contemplation time when I meditate and do some spiritual reading—a ritual that resonates with me and takes into account different religious traditions. This reminds me daily that connecting to my inner being in my own authentic way feels better than replicating traditional practices that may be preferred by others.

- The brief opportunity I have to connect with my husband on our daily commute every morning, a routine that ten years ago would have seemed like a far-fetched fairy tale because our union is almost a microcosm of the implicit and explicit tensions that can exist between families of different faiths. And the daily connecting makes me realise the little things that I love about him—the silly way he can make me laugh at a random joke, his determination to make a difference at work, and sometimes even the "guidance" he gives on how to navigate traffic, making me try things out of my comfort zone.

- My commute to work, which I try to make more pleasant (versus yelling at people in traffic) by a) catching up with my closest friends about things as small as what was on television last night to issues as heavy as what we are insecure about and will need to confront. On a hands-free device, of course; b) mindfully admiring the beautiful scenery peppered along the side of the road, such as wild flowers mixed in with cherry blossoms; or c) listening to books on tape, which keep me engaged and intrigued on my ride to work (so much so that I occasionally sit and continue listening to the audio book long after I have reached my destination).

- The contribution that I can make in my professional role, by being a positive person at work, staying passionate about the cause and constantly putting my best foot forward regardless of the task at hand. It is not always easy to see how a powerpoint presentation or an excel model that I have developed is connected to the broader mission of saving lives through the medicines we are discovering. But I am thankful for the opportunity to do my part.

- Tiny "setbacks" at work such as water spilling on my computer while I am working on an important deadline; I see these as opportunities to realise that I was probably taking things too seriously and need to calm down (though getting to that realisation generally takes longer!). It also makes me better appreciate my usually handy computer and I am thankful for the times that it has functioned seamlessly.

- Coming home daily to a place that I adore and that has remained as I had left it in the morning—it has yet to be consumed by fire despite my dangerous attempts at learning how to cook! I do not take for granted the fact that I have a safe roof over my head when I hear about the devastation of people who have lesser means or those suffering from the loss of their homes or loved ones through natural disasters, political situations or other events beyond their control.

- The food I have for dinner, because not only does it give me sustenance and energy, it also reminds me how my parents are spoiling my husband and I by sending us home-cooked meals almost on a weekly basis. These meals are akin to receiving love from our families, who communicate their affection by cooking and sharing delights that nourish our bodies and souls.

- The mindless television, music or books that I get to drown myself in at night as a bit of relaxation and play at the end of a busy day.

- My bed, which is truly warm and comforting, especially during cold nights which are not atypical in San Francisco.

- The fact that everyone I care about has been kept safe and secure as we go through our lives and try to make our own contributions for another day.

This daily practice allows me to count my blessings very easily and realise how fortunate I am. It also allows me to get snippets of energy throughout the day so that I have the willpower to tackle the challenges that come my way—either by trying to view them as opportunities or turning to the things that are going well as pillars of support.

It is also a good way to be mindful of the little lessons and adventures that life offers—how I behave in tough situations with a team member whom I may not see eye to eye with; how my stereotype about the homeless is challenged by someone I meet through my volunteering activities; or the realisation from the smile of a woman working in our building that sometimes, all it takes is a kind word to warm the heart of someone else, however brief the moment, however nameless they may remain.

There have been studies that show that optimism is something that can be learned partially through how we frame situations in our life. I believe this practice of being grateful will allow me to become a more optimistic, patient and mindful person—character traits that I would like to continue developing as my life unfolds in unexpected, but hopefully meaningful, ways.

• • •

Zeryn Mackwani Sarpangal is a Pakistani-American brought up in a Muslim family. Against the norm, she married her long-time love, an Indian-American from a Hindu family. Her decision epitomises a wider outlook in life, that everyone has a choice to make good their own lives and pursue happiness and meaning. She currently lives in the Bay Area in California, USA with her husband and near both their families and close friends.

ABOUT THE EDITORS

Pepukaye Bardouille was born in Dominica, but spent her formative years in Zambia and England. She studied engineering in America and France, and earned a doctorate in Energy and Environmental Systems Studies from Lund University in Sweden. Giving in to wanderlust, Pep has worked in Africa, Asia, Europe and the Middle East as both a management consultant and with international development agencies on corporate strategy, energy and sustainable development issues. Her interests are eclectic, but perhaps more than anything, she is happiest simply connecting with people, ideally while collecting random adventures from places near and far with her trusted camera in tow.

Neo Gim Huay was born and raised in Singapore. She studied engineering in Cambridge University and completed her MBA in Stanford University, spending close to a decade in public service before becoming an international management consultant. Gim Huay spent the last three years in Lagos, where she was both challenged and enriched by the dynamism and complexities of Nigeria living—with never a dull moment. Gim Huay now resides in Singapore. Eternally grateful for the opportunities that life has given her, the number one item on her bucket list is to give back to life multiple times more than what life has given her.